HAUSSMANN:
PARIS TRANSFORMED

PLANNING AND CITIES
(titles published to date)

VILLAGE PLANNING IN THE PRIMITIVE WORLD
  Douglas Fraser
CITIES AND PLANNING IN THE ANCIENT NEAR EAST
  Paul Lampl
URBAN PLANNING IN PRE-COLUMBIAN AMERICA
  Jorge Hardoy
MEDIEVAL CITIES
  Howard Saalman
THE RENAISSANCE CITY
  Giulio C. Argan
THE MODERN CITY: PLANNING IN THE 19TH CENTURY
  Françoise Choay
HAUSSMANN: PARIS TRANSFORMED
  Howard Saalman
**MILITARY CONSIDERATIONS IN CITY PLANNING:
  FORTIFICATIONS**
  Horst de la Croix
TONY GARNIER: THE CITÉ INDUSTRIELLE
  Dora Wiebenson
LE CORBUSIER: THE MACHINE AND THE GRAND DESIGN
  Norma Evenson

PLANNING AND CITIES

General Editor

GEORGE R. COLLINS, Columbia University

HAUSSMANN:
PARIS TRANSFORMED

HOWARD SAALMAN

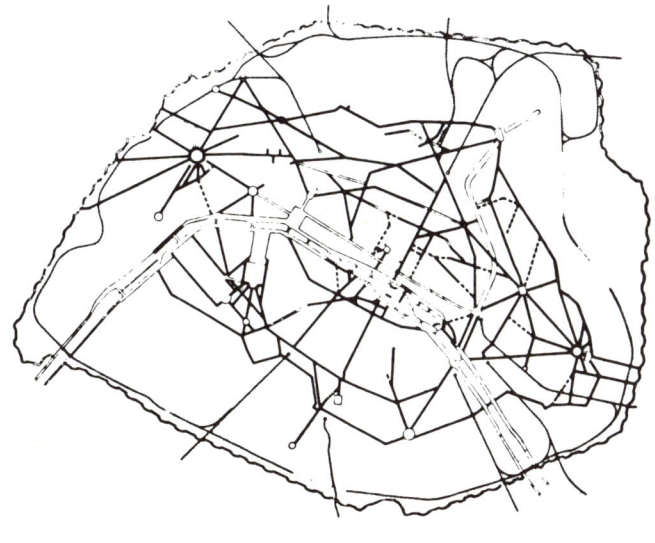

GEORGE BRAZILLER   NEW YORK

Copyright © 1971 George Braziller, Inc.
Published simultaneously in Canada by
Doubleday Canada, Limited.
All rights reserved
For information address the publisher:
George Braziller, Inc.   One Park Avenue   New York, N.Y. 10016
Library of Congress Catalog Card Number: 76–143399
Standard Book Number: 0–8076–0582–4 (paperbound)
              0–8076–0583–2 (hardbound)
Printed in the U.S.A.
First Printing

CONTENTS

General Editor's Preface   6

Preface   7

INTRODUCTION   8

THE REBUILDING OF PARIS, 1852–1870   14

   Streets   14

   Buildings, Politics, and Aesthetics   15

   Parks and Promenades   18

   Services   19

   Money   20

CRITICAL EVALUATION: 1   25

MEDIEVAL PARIS   29

PARIS FROM 1500 TO NAPOLEON III   34

CRITICAL EVALUATION: 2   46

PARIS SINCE HAUSSMANN   116

Illustrations   49

Notes   118

Dates of Persons and Reigns Mentioned in the Text   120

Bibliography   121

Index   123

Sources of Illustrations   128

GENERAL EDITOR'S PREFACE

The transformation of Paris was undoubtedly the most copied and yet controversial work of city planning in modern times. It drew on Baroque precedents and transformed them, ruthlessly, to fit the exigencies of rapid urbanization in an industrial age. It reflected the aspirations of a new business-minded upper middle class, and for these entrepreneurs it opened up the old city to the demands of modern commerce and transportation.

Our author projects the work of Haussmann and Napoleon III against the long history of the growth and urban renewal programs of Paris since early medieval times and argues that despite the criticism that their high-handed methods may have provoked, the two leaders succeeded in preserving and enhancing the viability of that city for several succeeding generations. They tapped its centers of rich activity, they aerated its noisome quarters, and they produced internal landscapes of an unprecedented scale that the Impressionists flocked to paint as enthusiastically as beaches, rivers, and rolling fields.

This is one of the volumes in our Planning and Cities series that concentrates on particular planners and cities. We expect that in the near future our books on Haussmann, Garnier, and Le Corbusier will be joined by studies of Ledoux, Olmsted, and others. Most of the volumes in the series have dealt with epochs or areas, and we are preparing others of that type to treat the classical period, the twentieth century, planning in socialist Eastern Europe, and the Orient.

G.R.C.

PREFACE

The Second Empire and the physical transformation of Paris by Napoleon III and his Parisian prefect, Georges-Eugène Haussmann, have been the subject of increasing interest and discussion on the part of historians and urban planners alike (*Fig. 1*). David Pinkney's excellent study, *Napoleon III and the Rebuilding of Paris* (see Bibliography), has provided the scholarly basis for further analysis. In returning to the subject in the Planning and Cities series, I am not attempting to expand the framework of factual historical data, but rather to reexamine the results of the Napoleonic program from different perspectives. If some well-known aspects of Haussmann's Paris as well as of the Paris of French kings from Louis VI to Louis Philippe come to appear in a new light, this book will have fulfilled its purpose.

    The various parts of this study are the product of several years of discussions with students in seminars on the history of cities. Paris, rich in urban developments during all major periods since antiquity, was a natural subject for investigation. The resulting ideas first took public form as the Walter W. S. Cook Alumni Lecture, under the title "Haussmann's Paris Revisited," held at the Institute of Fine Arts of New York University in May, 1967. It has been the custom for the Institute to publish these lectures with the aid of a generous bequest from an anonymous donor. The author, the general editor, and the publisher are grateful to the Institute and to its director, Craig Hugh Smyth, for permission to include this volume in the present series, thus making it available to the widest possible public.

    The publisher and his assistants have been most helpful in procuring the illustrations, for which I express my appreciation. To the tireless general editor of this series, George R. Collins, goes my boundless thanks for his unfailingly sure instinct in generously extending that most valuable aid to errant authors: constructive criticism.

H.S.

Carnegie-Mellon University
Pittsburgh, Pa.

INTRODUCTION

One hundred years ago the bourgeois empire of Napoleon III was approaching its demise. It was an era in which the fate of nations was decided by a ruler's ability to transform the fruits of the social, political, and industrial revolutions of the late eighteenth century into effective instruments of national power. The bid of the first Napoleon had been crushed in large measure by a rapidly industrializing England which was in the process of evolving socially and politically and emerging as a world power. The defeat of the later Napoleon by a newly unified and industrially potent Germany (*Fig. 2*), if not as dramatic, was nonetheless equally decisive for the future of Europe. The balance of power had been radically disturbed, with ominous consequences for coming generations.

The great political upheavals of the late eighteenth and early nineteenth century in the newly formed United States of America, in France, England, South America, and elsewhere had been essentially bourgeois revolutions. The bourgeoisie led the revolutions, took the reins of power, and kept them. Farmers who arrived in Paris singing the "Marseillaise" may not immediately have grasped the realities of the situation, but they had come to the city to stay on, to work alongside the older artisan classes in the mills and shops of the new industrial apparatus created by the bourgeoisie.

By name, by definition, and by tradition the bourgeois was a creature of the city. He had created it—sometimes with, other times without, the compliance of an aristocracy of feudal origins and of a church whose theological imperatives sanctioned a system of law and privilege that circumscribed and limited production and trade and, consequently, urban development. In the final analysis the great bourgeois revolution was a decisive blow in the long struggle between town and country that had been waged in Europe since the revival of urban production and trade in the eleventh century. It was a struggle that the city was winning.

A revolution that destroyed the social, political, and legal underpinnings of the order preceding it needed theoreticians and planners to prepare a blueprint for the new society-in-the-making, and firm executors to bring it about. The eighteenth century suffered from no shortage of either men of reason or men of action. Voltaire, Diderot, Rousseau, Jefferson, Hamilton, and Adam Smith drew the philosophical, political, and economic outlines: Man, in short, was created by God, but within that creation he was a being of reason, capable of shaping his environment in a rational form and measure and of ruling himself through a government of men with delegated powers, by and for the people. All men were created equal. Reason made man free to choose and shape his lot for better or worse. His rights to act within the law, to create freely, to own, and to sell what he had made or acquired were inalienable. The revolutionary armies under Napoleon I carried the new system across Europe. Ledoux, Boullée, Durand, Percier, and Fontaine in France; Schinkel, Gärtner, Klenze, Friedrich Weinbrenner in Germany; John Nash in England; and, of course, Thomas Jefferson in the United States, all gave the revolution architectural expression.

The state as the ultimate instrument and master of its newly created citizens was in the ascendancy: its prerogatives were less limited than even a Louis XIV dreamed of. With the middle class in command, the urban needs of the mercantile class required and would get urgent attention. The new order needed a new urban framework. What remained of the medieval, Renaissance, and Baroque nuclei of the cities—and a good deal remained—was not, in itself, sufficient for the new age. The times required more and larger buildings for governmental legislation, justice, and administration; buildings of public utility such as covered markets and market streets; hospitals, prisons, schools, institutions of every kind; and ever more barracks for the standing national armies. The need grew for new housing for the rising middle class; new public theaters and opera houses other than the aristocratic palace theaters where the arts had previously been nurtured; and museums designed not only for aesthetic enjoyment but for instruction in patriotic values. Sculpture galleries had pride of place in the new museums and displayed the great men of past and present in white togaed splendor, for instance, Karl Friedrich Schinkel's Altes Museum in Berlin, Leo von Klenze's Glyptotek in Munich, and Rafaelle Stern's new wing of the Vatican galleries.

The eighteenth-century town of Karlsruhe, capital of the small German principality of Baden, as expanded by Weinbrenner in the first two decades of the nineteenth century, is a uniquely complete example of what might be called the "ideal city of the bourgeois revolution" (*Figs. 3–4*). It had a central street and a succession of geometrically regular plazas comprising markets, a town hall, churches of all denominations, even a synagogue for the Jews recently liberated from the ghettos, theater, opera house, museum, barracks, and houses in all sizes and values from a palace of the Crown Prince (rubbing shoulders with the middle class) to the small merchant's shop and house off the main street.

While the revolutionary planners visualized some of the components required for the cities of the new order, they did not—probably could not—foresee the most significant consequence of the changes they helped to bring about: the enormous increase in population which followed the Industrial Revolution. The Karlsruhe plan typifies an almost universal characteristic of the early postrevolutionary town schemes: their relatively small scale. The urban ideal of the new planners—Jefferson is an example—seems to have been that whereas the middle class, founded on trade in the products of artisans, farmers, and small manufacturers, would now receive its just due, the size of the towns would remain within modest limits. Mechanization of industry and agriculture through the newly developed steam engines and similar inventions would leave the producers more leisure for the enjoyment of the arts and sciences which ennobled their existence. Nothing better illustrates this "unproblematic" conception than Ledoux's project for the industrial village of Chaux (*Figs. 5–6*). It featured little smoke and dirt, and proposed extravagant projects for physical and spiritual elevation around the edges. The furnaces of the forging plant seem almost more symbolic than functional. The projected population density was minimal.

The future turned out to be something quite different, and one can hardly blame the urban planners of the late eighteenth century for not anticipating it. The greater speed of production made possible by mechanization quickly increased the numbers who earned their living from the machine. By 1850 the population living in cities had doubled, a spurt unmatched since the previous urban explosion in the thirteenth century.[1] Accompanying social problems were also of unprecedented proportions: rapidly built housing of poor quality, overcrowding, disease, an appalling mortality in cities unequipped for the new scale of production and population. The contrast between a bygone age and modern times was too striking to pass unnoticed. There seemed to be no simple answers, and an entire school of English and European Romantics reacted by turning to neomedieval rusticity. This was facing the problem by avoiding it. But the need for positive response existed, and practical men would have to look in other directions to find it, or lose out in the struggle for political power.

The most influential nineteenth-century solution to the problem of the mushrooming city was Napoleon III's project for the rebuilding of Paris (*Fig. 7*), executed by his loyal assistant, the Prefect of the Department of the Seine and Imperial Baron, Georges-Eugène Haussmann (1809–1891). Some aspects of the project antedated the Second Empire, and Napoleon III himself developed its basic concepts of arterial streets and parks. Haussmann, however, not only added essential concomitant features such as a new water supply and sewer system but organized the scheme's complicated execution and intricate financing. Furthermore, since many of the aesthetic elements of the completed project are also his, it is both convenient and to an extent legitimate to speak of Haussmann's Paris.

The story has been told repeatedly, first by Haussmann himself in his three volumes of *Mémoires*, written after his forced retirement from public life and published in 1890–1893. A mixture of personal apologetics, political nostalgia, and not unmerited self-satisfaction, Haussmann's memoirs are a basic source of information, but a critical evaluation of his work and times must be founded on a more general reading of contemporary sources. Pinkney has done so, carefully analyzing the political, financial, and technical aspects of Haussmann's operations.[2] Haussmann's co-workers, Adolphe Alphand and Eugène Belgrand, produced monumental publications documenting their respective contributions to the creation of new parks and to the construction of the great water supply and sewer system.[3]

Nineteenth-century France presented a spectrum of political options following the first Napoleonic empire. At one end the unreconstructed monarchists refused to acknowledge the irrevocable consequences of political and industrial change and dreamed of the restoration of the old order under the aegis of a monarch whose guarantee of virtue would lie in his unimpeachably legitimate descent from the late royal line. Their political expectations were meager and their ultimate failure predictable. At the other extreme the socialist radicals viewed a republican government as only the first stage in the fundamental transformation of society, a process without which the revolutionary ideals of justice, equality, and brotherhood would not be realized. Their political hopes lay largely with the urban proletariat which the political and industrial revolutions had fostered but which the resulting political systems (republics or constitutional monarchies) had methodically ignored or repressed. Their prospects were limited by the fact that their proletarian constituents were interested less in a radical overturn of the existing system than in getting a larger share of its benefits. Between these extremes stood the majority of Frenchmen—independent farmers, small businessmen in Paris and the provinces, and the nascent group of industrial entrepreneurs. As a group this majority demanded the fulfillment of the bourgeois political, social, and economic demands that had been a major moving force of the revolution of 1789 and that had been delayed in the aftermath of the Napoleonic Wars.

Following the elimination of the restored Bourbon monarchy, dedicated to immobility and reaction, in the revolution of July 1830, came Louis Philippe's constitutional monarchy which supported middle class political stability and conservatively paced economic growth. The construction of railroads, begun and fostered during the July Monarchy (1830–1848), furthered the distribution of industrial products throughout the country and the movement of workers from the provinces to the growing metropolis (*Fig. 8*). But if urban shopkeepers and the provincial *petite bourgeoisie* found the pace comfortable, the rapidly rising upper middle class of manufacturers, high-powered merchants, and daredevil financiers in Paris and the growing provincial cities such as Lyons, Marseilles, and Bordeaux felt increasingly constricted by the régime's conservative economic and financial policies.

Paris in 1850 was hopelessly unequipped for the pace of the activities and the style of life to which the rising upper middle class aspired (*Fig. 12*). The July government had taken only a few limited steps toward the city's transformation, and its only major contribution was the relatively short stretch of the Rue de Rambuteau connecting the eastern quarters with Les Halles. New railroad terminals (*Fig. 9*) were built, quite logically, at the then-existing periphery of Paris, but access from them to the city center led through the tightly knit fabric of the old city, disruption of which required a kind of ruthless political initiative that the 1830 government was not prepared to take on a large scale. The dissatisfaction of the upper middle class, added to the increasing discontent of the urban workers, spelled the eventual end of the Louis Philippe monarchy.

When the revolution came in 1848 it was spearheaded by the Parisian proletariat (*Fig. 10*). Its radical leaders aimed beyond the reestablishment of a republican government toward a socialist restructuring of society. The majority of Frenchmen had no such aspirations, and the radical movement was quickly and bloodily immobilized. But there were men in France who saw the future in terms neither of popular democracy nor of the limited parliamentary government dear to the *petite bourgeoisie*. Combining a driving faith in scientific progress, industrial development, and commercial expansion with a sense for the application of the deficit financing economics of the Comte Claude Henri de Saint-Simon, this diverse group of industrial and financial managers, military men, publicists, and government administrators shared the romantic aura of bygone days of Napoleonic glory, of a France sure of itself and ready for great initiatives. The man who embodied all the strengths and weaknesses of this imperialist direction was the late Bonaparte's nephew, Louis Napoleon (Napoleon III, 1808–1873; *Fig. 11*). After decades in prison and exile during the Bourbon and Orléans régimes, his star rose with the rising hopes of the upper middle class in the wake of the 1848 revolution. His election as President of the 1848 republic, his *coup d'état* of 1852, and his proclamation of the Second Empire set the political stage for far-reaching changes.

Georges-Eugène Haussmann was made to order for this régime. Of Alsatian Protestant origins, he was born in Paris in 1809, the son of a Napoleonic officer. As a favor to his maternal grandfather, General Georges Dentzel (military governor of Vienna in 1809), Napoleon's stepson, Prince Eugène Beauharnais, acted as his godfather. This imperialist childhood remained a cherished memory. While his father engaged in moderate opposition to the restored Bourbons, Georges received his education at the Collège Henri IV and the Collège Bourbon, taking a doctorate in law at the École de Droit in 1831. While at law school he dabbled in music as an amateur instrumentalist and attended courses at the Conservatoire at the time Berlioz was a student there under Luigi Cherubini, but this modest artistic interest seems to have left few traces in his later life. Also at law school he participated in a minor way in the revolution of July 1830, receiving a slight wound in a skirmish with royal troops. He entered the public administration at the bottom of the ladder in 1831 and served at a succession of minor posts in western and central France. His rise under the conservative Orléans régime was far from meteoric. When the monarchy fell seventeen years later he was sub-prefect at Blaye near Bordeaux. His years in the lower echelons had strengthened the dominant aspects of his character: nagging ambition, indomitable self-confidence, a sense of the power inherent in a government administrator, a distaste for the political compromises required by parliamentary government, the ability to reduce the varied and complex problems of government to simple orderly categories, and an utter absence of scruples or doubt concerning the advantages of any project he had determined to carry out. His major weaknesses were an almost total inability to arrive at diplomatic compromises and an excessive dependence on the good will of his superiors; these failings initially recommended him to Louis Napoleon and the interior minister, the Duc de Persigny, almost as much as his strengths, but they ultimately hastened Haussmann's political demise.

After helping to carry the Gironde for Napoleon III in the presidential elections of 1848, Haussmann finally rose to the rank of prefect, serving successively in districts of the Var, the Yonne, and the Gironde. In 1852 he was prefect at Bordeaux when Napoleon proclaimed the Second Empire there. In 1853 he was called to assume the prefecture of the Seine and the task of restructuring Paris.

THE REBUILDING OF PARIS, 1852–1870

The great project developed by Napoleon III and Haussmann comprised four interrelated parts: streets, buildings, parks, and services. Each requires consideration.

STREETS

Earlier transformations of Paris had always consisted of additions to the already existing urban fabric (pp. 29–44). Napoleon III's idea of restructuring the city by cutting streets through it represented a fundamental change of approach, one suggested perhaps by Wren's plan for the rebuilding of London after the 1666 fire (*Fig. 13*), which had been cautiously applied in John Nash's Regent Street project earlier in the century.[4] The Rue de Rambuteau, built under the July Monarchy, had been a first timid Parisian step in this direction (*Fig. 14*). The projected network of arterial streets—drawn on a map of the city in different colors according to their urgency—which Napoleon III outlined to Haussmann in 1853 expanded this new approach to mid-nineteenth-century demands and expectations (*Figs. 7, 15*).

These streets had a twofold character: They existed both for their own sakes, as places to live and shop according to new standards of upper middle class affluence, as a kind of stage for elegant living, promenading, and socializing in outdoor cafés and restaurants, and also as connecting corridors between what an up-to-date mid-nineteenth-century man such as Napoleon III considered key points of the city (*Figs. 16–17*). As links the streets functioned in two directions: They provided rapid access from the railway stations at the city's then periphery to the key points at the center (government buildings, central markets, hospitals, business and entertainment districts), and in turn linked the central organs of administration and business (fire department, riot police, ambulance service, department store deliveries) with the focal points of the city's various quarters. The intersections of two or more such arteries would clearly become major nodes of traffic and urban activity.

Such considerations determined the location and direction of the new streets (*Figs. 15, 18*). Extension of the Rue de Rivoli to the Rue St.-Antoine, thus opening across the city an east-west axis from the Étoile to the Bastille, had already been started before Haussmann's administration. Now a north-south boulevard was to stretch southward from the Gare de l'Est between the old Rue St.-Martin and Rue St.-Denis and across the Ile de la Cité and the Left Bank to the end of the Jardin du Luxembourg where a short trunk avenue on axis with the Palais du Luxembourg would lead to the Observatoire. A secondary north-south avenue, the Rue de Rennes, would connect the Gare de Montparnasse at the southern end of the city with the center of the Left Bank at the old abbey of St.-Germain-des-Prés. The already existing boulevards marking the line of walls demolished by Louis XIV and making the circuit from the Place de la Concorde to the Bastille formed an inner ring, completed by the construction of the Boulevard St.-Germain, which also forms the main inner east-west route on the Left Bank. Diagonal avenues such as the Avenue Napoleon (now Avenue de l'Opéra) and the Rue de Turbigo were to connect important points already existing or yet to be created (the Louvre, Opéra, Les Halles or central markets, and so on). Secondary streets would link the main boulevards with key institutions located away from the major arteries (Rue des Halles, Rue du Pont Neuf, Rue des Écoles, Rue Soufflot, Rue du 4 Septembre, and so on). The exterior boulevards, only partially completed under the Second Empire, formed an outer ring comprising a secondary network of new streets which provided rapid access through and around the major *faubourgs*. In the east a triangle of avenues converged on the Place de la Nation; in the west radial avenues were developed around the Place de l'Étoile; in the north the Rue Lafayette (partially of earlier nineteenth-century origins) connected the Opéra intersection with the Gare du Nord and Gare de l'Est and continued northeastward out of the city; in the south the Boulevard Raspail linked the western end of the Boulevard St.-Germain with the Porte d' Orléans; and in the northwest the Boulevard Malesherbes connected the periphery with the business quarter around the Rue St.-Honoré–Rue Royale intersection.

The realization of these new streets cutting through old quarters involved extensive expropriation and demolition of private buildings. This crucial aspect could not be carried out without a plan of Paris drawn to the most exact scale. A Paris which had grown by gradual addition did not need and had not supplied such a plan. Haussmann needed it and with his customary efficiency organized a Service du Plan de Paris under his chief surveyor, the trustworthy Deschamps. Towers were set up around the town and the necessary survey produced by triangulation, a job which took a year.

BUILDINGS, POLITICS, AND AESTHETICS

Haussmann's success as an administrator was based on his aptitude for reducing the complex governmental tasks of his day to a limited number of clearly defined projects capable of realization. His success in carrying out the imperial program for Paris would have been much less if he or the government he served had been deeply concerned with catering to the wide variety of social, political, and cultural strata composing the nation. Such concern would have required nothing less than democratic give-and-take at all political levels, taking into account all the obstacles which the consequent political compromises would have posed to large-scale, single-minded solutions. Except for concessions to the Church in the form of publicly supported denominational schools along with secular schools, the Empire neglected this political approach almost by definition. The new Paris visualized by Napoleon III and by Haussmann was to be first a city useful to the political interests that the Empire represented above all others, a city whose social ethos, combining economic liberalism with political conservatism, could be summed up: as much as possible for the people, as little as possible by the people. If the rapidly expanding economy fostered by the Empire provided a vast number of new jobs, thus keeping the peasants who were streaming to the cities content and off the barricades, so much the better. If social benefits in the form of an expanded public school system, extensive parks, new sewers and waterworks, improved health and recreation facilities, filtered down to the lower middle and working classes, no harm done. If trade unions (permitted in 1864) helped to keep industrial peace, so be it. But all these benefits were part of an overall program geared primarily to the needs and objectives of the upper middle class in power.

Haussmann's "urban aesthetics" were nothing more or less than an expression of this basic ideal vision. A metropolis focused visually and functionally on major institutions such as the railway stations, the Tribunal de Commerce, the Hôtel du Louvre (under private management), Charles Garnier's new opera house, the city hall, the cathedral, and the former monastery of St.-Germain-des-Prés, represents the kind of conceptual simplification by which bureaucrats such as Haussmann could come to terms with the complexities of urban life at mid-nineteenth century, by which they gained self-assurance and the optimistic conviction that the new industrialized society could actually be governed and its problems managed if not wholly resolved.

The formal concept of linking major architectural units by grand avenues (*Fig. 16*), of superimposing a simplex of monumental proportions over a complex of smaller units, has Baroque precedents, particularly Wren's plan, in which radical avenues broken by "star" plazas link St. Paul's Cathedral with the Royal Exchange and the Tower while similar streets converge on the Exchange from the London Bridge and the main tower gates (*Fig. 13*). As applied in Paris of the Second Empire the old concept had new implications.

Some of the functional and symbolic units of the new Paris were already in existence (railway stations, the National Assembly, Bourse, Madeleine and Rue Royale complex, Panthéon, Notre-Dame, an enlarged Hôtel de Ville, Arc de Triomphe, Colonne de la Bastille, and so on). Others had yet to be created or re-created (Les Halles, ministries, courts, hospitals, new opera house, new barracks, fire stations, police stations, secular and denominational public schools, *mairies* for the old and new *arrondissements* of the growing city, theaters, and so on), and still others such as the Louvre, the Université, and the Palais de Justice required enlargement to function on a new scale. Some existing units such as the Arc de Triomphe, Notre-Dame, and the fragmentary tower of the old church of St.-Jacques-la-Boucherie (Tour St.-Jacques) were isolated in geometrically ordered open spaces surrounded by Second Empire institutional and apartment buildings.

Haussmann's penchant for lining up boulevards on buildings and monuments of varying proportions and importance has been much discussed.[5] The focus has been on aberrations such as the insignificant dome of the Tribunal de Commerce *(Fig. 20)*, which was deliberately displaced to the west side of the building to form a more or less effective visual termination for the Boulevard Sébastopol, or the alignment of the Boulevard Henri IV and the Pont Sully on the Colonne de la Bastille at one end and on the dome of the Panthéon at the other, although the boulevard does not extend to the Panthéon but swerves off to the west at the foot of the Left Bank to form the Boulevard St.-Germain.

The transformation of small-scale complexity into monumental simplicity was carried to its extreme consequences on the Ile de la Cité *(Figs. 19–20)*. Between 1853 and 1870 Haussmann changed this bustling core of the old city—containing a score of churches and monasteries, some 14,000 inhabitants, and a tight network of dozens of streets, alleys, and quays crowded between the cathedral and the old royal palace—into an institutional center comprising the gigantic Palais de Justice (built into the old royal palace), the Tribunal de Commerce, the central hospital (Hôtel Dieu), the now wholly isolated cathedral without its former cloisters and without the former archbishop's palace, and several large barracks (one of which later became the Prefecture of Police). A small fragment of residential streets remained at the northeast corner of the island; the truncated triangular Place Dauphine (see pp. 34–36), whose eastern side had to make way for the great new wing of the Palais de Justice, survived at the western end. The Pont Neuf also remained, more indispensable than ever as part of the second major east-west crossing at the center of town. Thoroughly overhauled by Eugène Emmanuel Viollet-le-Duc and separated from its former urban context by the gigantic rectangular Place du Parvis in front and by a pleasant little park on the side and in back, Notre-Dame became somewhat less the town cathedral and rather more a national monument and a central object of the increasingly popular cult of French historical reminiscence in which Gothic architecture and the Paris cathedral in particular played an important role (for instance in Victor Hugo's *Notre Dame de Paris*, first published in 1831).

Architectural, sculptural, and pictorial refinements were secondary in this transformation of Paris, and comparisons with the way such programs were carried out in the days of Louis XIV and Louis XV are not flattering to the new age. This was less a matter of parsimony than of taste; for the decoration of the expanded Hôtel de Ville, the new wings of the Louvre, and the new Opéra no expense was spared and the best available talent was hired. F.-J. Duban's wing of the École des Beaux-Arts (1860–1862) is a work of distinction and Henri Labrouste's great reading room at the Bibliothèque Nationale (1862–1868), a masterpiece. But the somewhat mechanical exuberance of the new Louvre pavilions (L.-T.-J. Visconti and H. M. Lefuel, 1852–1857; *Fig. 21*) and of Garnier's Opéra represent the essence of Napoleon III's conceptions of elegance and luxury.

Haussmann's approach to architectural design was characteristic: Its difficulties could be resolved by sound administration. Since Napoleon I's time, architects had been trained in both the École Polytechnique and the École des Beaux-Arts. Haussmann clearly leaned to the technical side. A well-organized Service d'Architecture with civil service status and fringe benefits would, he was certain, attract the best artistic talents. Although the artistic skill of the men involved in the Service was little better than average, Haussmann's bureaucratic control over his artistic subordinates occasionally had positive results. Victor Baltard, who had evolved a blockhouse-like design for the pavilions of Les Halles and had begun to erect the first of them (to the dismay of the inhabitants of the quarter who nicknamed the structure the "Fort des Halles") was forced to demolish it; pushed by Napoleon and Haussmann, he turned to the creative use of iron construction in the final project (*Fig. 22*) for which he later claimed exclusive credit.

PARKS AND PROMENADES

Surrounded and sustained as he was by men of affairs and technicians, Napoleon III was at heart a romantic, given to impulsive enthusiasms quickly followed by cautious retrenchment. Haussmann, usually eager to claim priority of conception for the various aspects of the Paris project, attributed the idea for the great park developments at the extremes of the city and for the various parklets throughout the center entirely to the Emperor. There is a hint of apology, almost of skepticism, as he outlines the expenditures for the parks. He makes it clear that he does not share the Emperor's *illusions généreuses* about the positive effects these parks will have on the morals and customs of the working classes. Commenting retrospectively in 1890, he notes that no such positive effects are discernible. However, as a convinced partisan of the believers in fresh air and sunshine as a means of preventing epidemic disease in crowded cities, he was willing to admit that such green areas and the trees planted along the new boulevards served a purpose.

Actually he was fascinated with the resolution of the formidable technical problems by the able park designer, Adolphe Alphand, and, being a practical administrator, he found it possible to justify the expenditures required for the artificial lakes, grottoes, waterfalls, greenhouses, and zoological gardens which delighted the Emperor and the public in terms of the rising land values around the parks and the increased revenues that resulted to the city. Further income came from the concessionaires and vendors who provided services and entertainment.

The Bois de Boulogne, a former royal hunting preserve, was the first object of attention (*Figs. 23–25*). With its lakes and promenades and the nearby Longchamps racetrack (developed on adjoining public land by a Jockey Club syndicate headed by the Emperor's stepbrother), it remains to this day the largest and most fashionable of Parisian parks. Similar parks at somewhat smaller scale but at no less cost were developed in the east (Bois de Vincennes, *Fig. 26*), the northeast (Buttes Chaumont), and the south (Montsouris), while in the northwest the Park Monceau, a refurbished former Orléans possession, became the focal point of the fashionable quarter developed by the real estate company controlled by the brothers Émile and Isaac Pereire, friends of Haussmann.

Whatever the depth of the Emperor's concern for the wretched poor, the new parks were a success in terms of practical politics and became one of the long-term accomplishments of the regime. Napoleon was lacking as a strategist and international diplomat, but he understood well what Frenchmen and women of all ages and classes enjoyed—after all, he was a Frenchman.

SERVICES

An expanding Paris enjoyed parks but the city also needed better illumination, fresh water, sewers (*Figs. 27, 29*), and adequate cemeteries. Haussmann provided ample gas lighting but, though usually attracted by technical innovations, he disliked and saw no future for electric lighting and regretted its introduction in the 1880's. Haussmann's chief of water services, Eugène Belgrand, has left his own documented account of the great aqueduct and sewer constructions carried out under the Empire. Here was a project closest to Haussmann's own preferences and capabilities, and its planning and realization remain among his most lasting accomplishments. Aided by the able Belgrand, Haussmann more than doubled the fresh water supply of the city by tapping sources as far as a hundred miles away in the Yonne (*Fig. 28*), Vanne, and Dhuis river valleys and by bringing the water to Paris on aqueducts unequaled since Roman times. The sewer system is no less impressive. A capillary network of street sewers emptied by gravitational action into large elliptical collectors' sewers which carried the drainage from all parts of the city northwestward to empty into the Seine at Asnières, well below Paris (*Fig. 30*). The sewers were accessible for easy maintenance and were cleaned with water-propelled mechanical devices. Haussmann had no new solution to the problem of eliminating human wastes which, fearful of contamination, he would not allow to flow into the sewer system. But he left Paris without stagnant water standing in the streets and with the flood danger appreciably reduced.[6]

Haussmann's penchant for mechanical solutions to large-scale problems led him to failure in resolving the cemetery question. Napoleon I's cemeteries of Montmartre, Père Lachaise, and Montparnasse, established just outside the then limits of the city, had been engulfed by the extension of the municipal limits in 1860 and were reaching their capacity. Haussmann viewed this as primarily a problem of sanitation to be resolved by a suitable technical solution. Characteristically, in 1864 he appointed a commission of engineers, including Belgrand, to find a proper location. The engineers favored a site at Méry-sur-Oise, some thirteen miles northwest of Paris. A single gigantic cemetery, to serve all of Paris, was to be connected with the city by a special funerary railway with departures from the three major cemeteries in the city. Insensitive to the negative psychological overtones of this "iron horse express to the grave" conception, Haussmann found himself unprepared for the popular outcry his proposal raised, and nothing finally came of it.

MONEY

The "Comptes fantastiques d'Haussmann" (the satiric title of a series of anti-Haussmann articles published in 1867 by Jules Ferry in the journal *Temps*)[7] became a political household word in the last years of the Empire, and it was the politics of money that eventually led to Haussmann's political decline. Charges of personal corruption could not be sustained against him: He was ambitious, arrogant, and susceptible to the spell of powerful men of business and government, but fundamentally honest. Aggrieved pride led him to refuse a generous imperial settlement upon his sudden resignation early in 1870. He did not effectively anticipate the rapid fall of his protector and had to live out his remaining twenty years on a modest prefectural pension and a small outside income.

It was not Haussmann's conduct but the economic and political guidelines of the Empire that were under attack in the late 1860's. Napoleon III had come to power during an economic recession. The *coup d'état* of 1852 and the proclamation of the Empire set off an economic boom that continued for well over a decade. But the imperial machine ran on an unstable mixture of credit: the propellant, shocking to conservative bankers and traditional economists, was deficit financing. Such financing of badly needed national investment in a time of rapidly expanding population and production is, to present-day economists nurtured on the teachings of Lord Keynes, quite justifiable. Its justification in the 1850's was the anticipation that the increased tax revenues accruing to the city from an expanding economy would suffice to pay off the long-term debts contracted for public works. The idea was current in Saint-Simonian circles around Napoleon III; Haussmann claimed (probably wishfully) to have originated it. The rapid expansion of industry and commerce was based on similar principles. Old-line bankers such as the Rothschilds backed off, but a new breed of enterprising financiers like the Pereire brothers and their bank, the Crédit Mobilier, which worked with capital drawn from small and large investors, jumped in with both feet. Their expectations were richly rewarded.

Haussmann began his financing with a series of municipal bond issues sold to the public at large, with venturesome banks taking the remainder. Such debentures, authorized by the legislature, covered only a small part of the projected outlays. The Emperor thereupon supported the creation of a Caisse des Travaux with limited funding and the authority to issue its own bonds to a limit of 100 million francs. This floating debt was not authorized by the legislature, but expenditures far beyond even this sum were on Haussmann's planning boards. For their realization he resorted to financial expedients completely beyond the control of the elected body and for some years kept so secret that, though not actually illegal, they gravely compromised Haussmann's position. Contracts were written which obligated the contractors not only to carry out the work but to pay compensation for expropriated property, in short to assume all financial burdens of the project. The contractors, naturally, did not have the capital to cover the costs which amounted to millions of francs. Just as naturally, banks would not advance such moneys to contractors on the strength of a city contract award alone. Haussmann's financial innovation lay in the expedient of formally considering a project "completed" before it was begun. This formality obligated the city to pay the contractor the agreed-upon sum in installments with interest and to give him negotiable bonds (so-called *bons de délégation*) in lieu of this obligation. The contractors, with Haussmann acting as intermediary, found little difficulty in persuading the government mortgage bank, the Crédit Foncier (whose director was favorable toward the imperial schemes for Paris), to advance the required funds in exchange for the *bons de délégation* which were accepted at discount, an advantageous affair for the bank since the city's credit was good and the risks small.

In practice the operation simply allowed the city to float a large debt without formal authorization from the legislative body, since the city merely undertook obligations while the contractors borrowed the money; but the necessary expedient of giving the contractors a legal claim against the city before any work was done was highly questionable. When one considers that by this method Haussmann raised half a billion of the two and one-half billion francs spent on the transformation of Paris during his time in office, whereas only roughly one-third of the total was covered by the surplus of rising city receipts over ordinary expenditures—the magic resource of the Saint-Simonists—it becomes clear why political trouble was bound to follow. The problem was not merely that the full extent of the work, particularly the enormous costs of aqueducts and sewers, had not been and could not be adequately foreseen but also that the very economic expansion stimulated by deficit financing released uncontrollable inflationary forces. All prices rose steeply in the decade after 1852, and the final costs of the vast construction projects far overshot all preliminary estimates. The cost of expropriation in particular, subject to political pressure and collusion, was higher than anticipated, and as a specifically public aspect of Haussmann's work it was open to constant criticism and comment. The expropriation juries, though guided by the appraisals of the incorruptible surveyor Deschamps, were often more than generous, and property owners resorted to all the devices common in such circumstances to increase their claims against the city. To some, left out of the pork barrel, it seemed as if there were no faster way to make a killing than to be expropriated. The big real estate operators, the Crédit Mobilier in particular, were quick to buy up all available property alongside the newly created boulevards, correctly anticipating the enormous rise in these properties' value as the new streets became the prime sites for fashionable residence and commerce.

In a final accounting, however, it must be acknowledged that Haussmann's ideas of deficit financing proved correct. The tax base of Paris grew along with the economic expansion made possible by the city's transformation, and surplus income eventually covered the outlay many times over. By the time of Haussmann's death in 1891, when the political clamor of the 1860's had died down, it was generally admitted that Paris could not only afford to do what was done, it could not have afforded *not* to do it.

There is another economic aspect of the transformation of Paris that should be emphasized. Although much has been written about the typical apartment houses which rose along Haussmann's boulevards (*Figs. 32, 82*), not enough importance has been given to the fact that all of this housing was built by private enterprise. In sheer volume this construction for elegant commercial buildings and upper middle class residences far outstripped the bulk of public work done in Haussmann's time and after. It is easy to sneer in retrospect at the greed for fast speculative profits which motivated the builders: undoubtedly fortunes were made (and sometimes lost) in real estate in those years. But what planner today can anticipate with equal assurance that the lots of his best urban projects will actually be built up with the required commercial and residential structures without investment of public funds? To be sure, the Napoleonic government encouraged such enterprise with tax exemptions and easy credit, but the very fact that so much was built so quickly to acceptable aesthetic and structural standards with private funds alone is proof of the fact that the Second Empire planners had correctly estimated both needs and possibilities in the second half of the nineteenth century.

"Need," urban or otherwise, can be variously defined. The lower social classes of Paris also needed a better city and a better life. Although they benefited directly from some of the Napoleonic projects such as parks, sewers, and schools, and significantly though indirectly from the seemingly endless opportunities for work which the Haussmann era created, it cannot be said that the Second Empire catered to the working classes as it did to its immediate clients, the upper middle class. The needs of a social group become an effective obligation on government only when backed up by political power which cannot be denied. The lower middle and working classes of France did not have the organized political power required, and the Second Empire found it possible to neglect their demands if not to ignore them altogether. How to convince the taxpaying segment of the population that tax money should be spent to satisfy the demands of the low or non-taxpaying segment remains a perennial political problem of all governments. Rather than condemning the Second Empire for its glaring political and social deficiencies, it seems more useful to point out that the upper middle class at mid-nineteenth century also had specific and undeniable "needs" involving the shape and character of their cities. They had the political and economic power to back up their demands; consequently their demands were met and their expectations fulfilled.

CRITICAL EVALUATION: 1

Sensational and controversial in its own time, Haussmann's great project not only spawned a school of Haussmann-inspired urban developments from Vienna to Barcelona and from Berlin to Rome[8] but has been the subject of continuing interest and discussion over the last fifty years. While the Second Empire style was strictly out of fashion during much of this time and has only recently received a balanced reassessment,[9] modern critics have treated Haussmann from their particular points of view.

There are nostalgic local historians who reject out of hand the Haussmannization of Paris as a mutilation of the old city with its historical associations, its intimacy, and its picturesque confusion.[10] Given the impact of recent influential studies with decidedly anti-bulldozer themes,[11] this point of view demands consideration.

Social critics of the urban scene, of both American democratic and European socialist orientations, are naturally unsympathetic to the social and political trappings of the Second Empire as such and, by association, to Haussmann's blatant catering to the ruling upper middle class. American writers such as Lewis Mumford,[12] committed to social improvement and mobility within the free workings of an expanding industrial and democratic society, want to see the city as an environment in which all members of that society can live and grow to the limit of their natural abilities amid fresh air and good schools, and can make the transition upward from the bottom of the social scale with a minimum of friction. These writers' ideal environment is suburban rather than urban: Haussmann's Paris, even with its parks and other urban facilities, does not meet this test.

Exponents of C.I.A.M. theories of city planning[13] are generally committed to progress, industrialization, mechanization, and large-scale urban transformation within a vaguely defined framework of socialist ideas tinged with occasional totalitarian overtones. They are bound to take Haussmann's efforts seriously, but their feelings are ambivalent. On one hand they see Haussmann as a nineteenth-century prophet of the new planned order, a forerunner of Tony Garnier and Le Corbusier. They are in sympathy with the strong technical flavor of his approach, with the grand scale of his conceptions, and with his quasi-dictatorial prerogatives. They like the scale and the iron construction of the new Halles, of Henri Labrouste's libraries, and of the new railroad stations. Gustave Eiffel's tower at the Paris Exhibition of 1889 in the Champ-de-Mars becomes a belated but fitting symbol for the whole era. In Haussmann's emphasis on broad streets between major points within the city they see a first recognition of the traffic problem and the precursor, albeit imperfect, of the parkways and superhighways of the future.

But Haussmann was unfortunately caught up in a world not yet ready for salvation. In spite of their secret admiration for the semi-autocratic features of the Second Empire that made his work possible, his critics are fundamentally out of sympathy with the France of Napoleon III and the nineteenth century in general. Sigfried Giedion viewed it as a time of "uncertainty," given to "dangerous expedients" without worthy social and political ideals or good architects. The transformation of Paris was "carried through by engineers." Napoleon was a political weakling who "drew up great schemes, but when serious difficulties arose . . . tried to twist his way through by making numerous petty concessions . . . to bargain his way out at the cheapest price." Haussmann was as a David fighting the Goliath of a short-sighted bourgeois opposition, but "as soon as he became a political storm center, Napoleon to all intents and purposes abandoned him."[14]

According to Giedion, what was right with Haussmann was due to the big scale, big planning, and engineering of his work. What was wrong was due to the bourgeoisie, bourgeois values, and "the split personality of the nineteenth century [which] appears in its almost inextricable mingling of constituent with transitory facts."[15] The boulevards may be fine for traffic, but Haussmann's critics cannot shake off a certain repugnance for their much trumpeted (and up to this day unproved) usefulness in suppressing popular insurrections. They mourn the defeat of the imperial project for an outer "greenbelt" around the perimeter of the expanded town.

They are most appalled by the basic unit of Haussmann's city, the new privately built apartment houses along the boulevards (*Fig. 32*),

> with shops on the ground floor, a mezzanine floor, three main floors and two attic floors. The three main floors have the same plan. They are apartments intended for upper middle class tenants. The three-windowed bedroom for Monsieur and Madame takes up the space at the corner. To its left is the living room, to the right the dining room. Further along to the right are the other bedrooms. There is a nursery which receives almost no light. The kitchen and the servant's room look onto a narrow light-well. These narrow light-wells are an evil characteristic of Continental dwelling houses of this period and of the years after it as well. The attic floors are the most densely overcrowded parts of the building. Here bed is placed next to bed, in the most confined space possible, for the accomodation of servants, night lodgers and the lower classes generally. . . . The uniform façade of this house of 1860 covers a living unit in which the most

> diversified functions of daily living swirl together. Business takes over the ground floor and often encroaches on the mezzanine, in workrooms connected with the various establishments. The three main floors are given over to apartments for the well-to-do. The attic floors are congested slums. In earlier times the association of production with dwelling quarters was quite natural, but . . . it is absurd in an age of industrial production to permit residence, labor and traffic to intermingle.[16]

This dislike of the Parisian apartment house extends to the total urban context as well. The boulevard becomes

> the endless street . . . that stretches beyond the range of the eye. [While] the neutral façades and the general uniformity make Haussmann's enormous work of rebuilding better than any other executed in or after the fifties of the nineteenth century . . . the most appalling disorder lies concealed . . . behind the uniform outer walls. . . . The street dominates contemporary bird's eye views of the city [*Fig. 76*]. The houses which do not front on it have plainly been allowed to spring up in a huddled confusion. Haussmann uses the uniform façade as a kind of wardrobe into which all disorder can be crammed.[17]

Haussmann planned to rid the town of the "dreadful infected alleyways and centers of epidemics" with which "the central part of Paris was littered," but "never really succeeded in cleaning up these areas, and the middle of Paris is still in bad condition."[18]

Is Haussmann to blame for all this? Not really: ". . . at the stage of social and industrial development that existed in Haussmann's day not even the beginnings of a solution to housing problems in great cities had been found." The bourgeoisie is the villain of the piece: "The bourgeoisie overthrew Haussmann . . . [it] could not forgive [him] for disturbing their peace. What he achieved was achieved against the will of the majority."[19]

There is an unspoken corollary to the criticism by Le Corbusier's disciples. Since they feel that society must be changed at its spiritual and physical roots, they tend to imply that an effective transformation of the city for the needs of the coming new day must begin by demolishing altogether the dead old heap of past urban mistakes.[20] It is not that Haussmann and Napoleon III went too far, but that they did not go far enough.

Common to all of these approaches is the tendency to take Haussmann's project out of context, as a kind of independent addition to the city. No one has thoroughly considered what is perhaps the most essential aspect of the program, namely its intimate relationship to the previously existing city. The criterion of urban success or failure in Haussmann's Paris is not, as we shall see, a matter of addition, but of integration.

Our evaluation must begin not with Haussmann's program and its theoretical and formal sources, but with a review of the history of Paris itself, a history that goes back some 1,500 years before Haussmann and contains a rich variety of urban experience which may help to explain the assurance and expertise with which Napoleon III and his Prefect of the Seine, neither one a trained architect or urban planner, approached their task.

MEDIEVAL PARIS

Cities, like people, prefer to attribute their present eminence to noble and ancient lineage, and Paris is no exception.[21] Yet when all is said and done, Gallo-Roman Lutetia Parisiorum, sometime residence of the fourth-century emperors Constantius Chlorus and Julian the Apostate did not amount to very much. Its few surviving monuments are concentrated on the slopes of the Mont. Ste.-Geneviève on the Left Bank. The Baths of Constantius Chlorus are, at best, a provincial version of Roman monumentality (*Fig. 31*). The Arènes de Lutèce, an amphitheater whose fragments were dug up during the Second Empire, is even less impressive.

The Merovingians withdrew to the Ile de la Cité which was fortified with a wall. The Left Bank was split up between the Benedictines of Ste.-Geneviève and of St.-Germain-des-Prés (*Fig. 33*). Much of the Right Bank became the property of the Bishop of Paris, ensconced in his cathedral church on the island. During the periods of Merovingian and Carolingian rule, the crown maintained only a small foothold at the western end of the island (*Fig. 34*). The Carolingians, land-centered rather than urban-centered, made little use of Paris. What attention they paid to the area was given to the royal abbey of St.-Denis to the north. A new highway (later the Rue St.-Denis) was built to the abbey from opposite the old Merovingian palace at the west end of the Ile de la Cité. The new river crossing, the Grand Pont at the head of the Rue St.-Denis, probably goes back to this period. The old Roman bridge at the head of the Rue St.-Martin was allowed to crumble away. Norman raiders came up the river, leaving the Parisian settlements in ruins. However, there was little in the way of a town to burn. A sometime royal residence, the nearby cathedral church of an episcopal see, and a few flourishing monasteries in the neighborhood, each surrounded by a small settlement, may yield some choice plunder, but they do not make a city.

By the end of the tenth century Hugh Capet and his successors were firmly entrenched in their island residence, and the city was changing rapidly. While the Left Bank, dominated by its fortified abbeys, continued in agricultural somnolescence, a market was founded before the end of the ninth century on the *Grève*, the sandy right bank opposite the Ile de la Cité and between the river and the east-west road along the shore. Across the wide arm of the river, not far from the site of the old Roman bridge (which, together with its shorter counterpart on the other side, the Petit Pont, had formed part of the main Roman north-south road from Senlis to Orléans), the Place de Grève and its adjoining parish church of St.-Gervais formed the nucleus of the first commercial center in Paris. Here, not on the island, was the beginning of modern Paris, and here its center remained.

By the eleventh century a similar center, no less important, had formed around the new parish church of St.-Jacques-la-Boucherie at the head of the Grand Pont (now Pont-au-Change), which connected the island with the Carolingian road to Saint-Denis. Before the middle of the twelfth century these two mercantile *faubourgs* were enclosed by a town wall. Just to the west a separate settlement had grown up around the parish church of the large episcopal domain on the Right Bank, St.-Germain-l'Auxerrois.[22] The outline of its *bourg* wall, preserved at least in name in the Rue des Fossés Saint-Germain, is still clearly discernible in surviving early-nineteenth-century plans of Paris, whereas the western curve of the eleventh–twelfth-century town enclosure can be traced from the Rue St.-Denis past the former cloister of St.-Opportune and down to the river along the Rue des Lavandières (*Fig. 18*). Not yet sufficiently developed commercially to force its inclusion or, perhaps, overly isolated by its wall, the Bourg Saint-Germain-l'Auxerrois remained cut off from the town, much as the abbey of St.-Germain-des-Prés on the other side of the river still was at the beginning of the seventeenth century (*Fig. 37*).

Under Louis the Fat the commercial pulse of the expanding city on the Right Bank quickened. In 1137 the market, grown too large for the Place de Grève and isolated by the disappearance of the old Roman bridge, was transferred to a new location just outside the eleventh–twelfth-century wall, along the Rue St.-Denis and next to the Cimetière des Saints-Innocents (*Fig. 34*). It was an historic move. The central market of Paris remained there until our own time. With its open marketplace, its covered market halls, and the surrounding market streets, Les Halles became the new focal point of the expanding city (*Fig. 36*).

By the end of the twelfth century an entire new cluster of *faubourgs* had sprung up. New streets had bridged the short gap between the early town and the Bourg Saint-Germain-l'Auxerrois. Toward the north there was the Bourg-Neuf Saint-Germain; the Bourg-le-Abbé around the monastery of St.-Magloire; the "Beaubourg" stretching from the parish church of St.-Merry, just inside the first wall, out to the Cluniac priory of St.-Martin-des-Champs, and over to the road connecting the early town with the fortified enclosure in which the Knights of the Temple (Templiers) had settled in the second half of the twelfth century (*Figs. 33–34*).

A group of parish churches grew up with the new quarters outside the wall. The merchants and artisans of the former *faubourgs* along the river's edge, turned *bourgeois* (in the literal sense of the word) by virtue of their wall, and the new *faubourgeois*, clamoring to be likewise included, were becoming the dominant force, the very *raison d'être* of the evolving city. In the early phases of urban growth they had been content to develop their own quarter and its church. Now their demands and their ambitions were rising. They wanted political organization and control over matters of common interest; they formed trade guilds. The *prévôt* of the oldest guild, the so-called water merchants who carried goods in barges up and down the river, became the *de facto* mayor of Paris. Equally, the bourgeois wanted visible participation in the representative life of the city. For the leading burghers, this meant church patronage with the right of burial in the cathedral or in the leading parish churches and abbeys around the city, previously an exclusive privilege of the feudal lords who literally owned the churches in their domains. The great new Cathedral of Notre-Dame, begun in 1163 and completed with its ring of chapels in the thirteenth century, was the ultimate fulfillment of these ambitions. Gothic architecture implies not only a larger scale and daring construction methods but also increasing—almost infinite—subdivision of the churches into ever smaller parts, giving formal and liturgical expression to the new complex of social and political realities in the towns. In the final analysis, Gothic architecture is architecture of the city, as Romanesque had been the architecture of feudalism. Not surprisingly, nearly all the Romanesque churches of Paris had been replaced by Gothic buildings before the end of the sixteenth century.

Not only the bishop, abbots, and clergy were happy to accommodate the flourishing merchants. The French crown as well realized early that its interests lay as much with the city as with the old feudal countryside. Adam Smith in the first and still classic disquisition on the "Rise of the Towns" stated the matter succinctly:

> The king . . . might despise [but] he had no reason either to hate or fear the burghers. Mutual interest, therefore, disposed them to support the king and the king to support them against the lords. They were the enemies of his enemies, and it was his interest to render them as secure and independent of those enemies as he could.[23]

The practical expression of this mutual interest was the great masonry wall of Paris, the first that also included the Left Bank, built by Philip Augustus around the year 1200 (*Figs. 34, 37*).

The reconstruction of eleventh- and twelfth-century Paris requires some archaeological imagination. The city which Philip Augustus enclosed with his wall, and which by the year 1300 had already spread northward beyond it, is preserved in numerous sixteenth- and seventeenth-century views and in some stubbornly lively surviving fragments of the wall (*Figs. 18, 37*).

The earlier Paris had been a patchwork of feudal estates. Its island center formed an almost classic representation of the Carolingian ideal: cathedral and palace, church and state in harmonic balance, dividing the power and the land between them (*Figs. 19, 37–38*). Monasteries and feudal retainers found their place in between. The merchants and artisans were left outside, huddled on the Right Bank, knocking at the bridgehead gates, biding their time.

The Paris of Philip Augustus, Saint Louis, and Philip the Fair took on a wholly new scale and harmony. Saint Louis enhanced the symbolic status of the palace and the monarchy with the acquisition of the Crown of Thorns and other major relics, which were spectacularly housed in the Ste.-Chapelle (1243–1246) in the palace courtyard (*Figs. 38–39*). But part of the palace also became the bureaucratic center for the administration of justice, the *parlement*, in which the townsmen had their voice. Although the Cathedral of Notre-Dame was still the bishop's church, the burghers shared in it also, and its form reflected their participation. The market and its great halls, the large Cimetière des Saints-Innocents which received the major share of generations of Parisians (*Figs. 34, 40*), the new large hospital opposite the cathedral, the Hôtel Dieu (*Figs. 19, 53*), and institutions outside the wall like the Hospice des Quinze-Vingts (*Figs. 18, 50*), a home for the blind founded by Saint Louis in 1260, are evidence that the city was gradually becoming more than a residence of bishop and king, but a functioning city for the merchants and artisans as well.

The most significant new feature of Paris in the thirteenth century was the enclosure and development of the *faubourg* on the Left Bank (*Fig. 37*). Of the old Benedictine abbeys founded by the Merovingians which had long dominated this area, St.-Genèvieve came just inside the new wall; St.-Germain-des-Prés, firm in its feudal prerogatives, remained outside.[24] The real impetus for the development of the south side, however, came not from the monasteries but from the numerous secular and religious *collèges* of the growing Université which began to spring up after 1200 on the relatively cheap land of the Left Bank (*Fig. 34*). Theology, law, science, and the conducting of business being inextricably intertwined in the late Middle Ages, the Université became the indispensable intellectual complement to the merchants' town on the other side of the river.

By the beginning of the fourteenth century something like a French national identity was forming around the symbol of the crown. But urban interests and national interests are not always identical, particularly if a national effort brings with it high taxes without the fruits of success. France's engagement in the early campaigns of the Hundred Years War (1337–1453) was less than successful. In 1356 John the Good was taken prisoner by the English on the field of Poitiers. Not long afterward, in 1358, Paris saw its first bourgeois revolution under the merchants' *prévôt*, Étienne Marcel. The revolution was repressed by the force of the crown, which had joined in an alliance of convenience with the landed nobles whose serfs were also in rebellion. Although Paris survived the turmoil with only a minimum of urban independence, it managed to acquire its first town hall, the Hôtel de Ville, on the Place de Grève (*Figs. 34, 41*). In the sixteenth century the early building was replaced by a larger structure (*Fig. 42*) which was enlarged after 1837 and rebuilt after burning by the Communards in 1870.

Charles V allowed the city few political liberties, but he did build a new wall on the busy northern side where the town had grown well beyond the wall of Philip Augustus. The fortress of the Bastille on the new wall (*Figs. 18, 43*) next to the new Porte Saint-Antoine was the complement to Philip Augustus' Louvre outside the Porte Saint-Honoré on the west (*Fig. 34*). If Philip Augustus had reason to fear attack from England, Charles was presumably worried about his ambitious brother, Philip the Bold. In the fifteenth century the English and the Burgundians attacked Paris from all directions. But the Bastille was even more useful in repressing the political ambitions of the Parisians themselves, as were the huge fortresses Charles had built at the heads of the Petit Pont and the Grand Pont (*Figs. 19, 34*).

PARIS FROM 1500 TO NAPOLEON III

By the end of the sixteenth century national, not urban, effort and interest was deciding the fate of Europe. The bourgeoisie of Paris returned to its alliance with an ever more absolute monarchy. The feudal nobility, effectively neutralized, no longer formed a serious obstacle to the royal power, which was now in a position to mobilize the resources of an entire country. The upper ranks of merchants and intellectuals joined the nobility as the *noblesse de robe* to provide the essential bureaucratic apparatus which kept the whole machine running.

Paris was divided into an urban nobility, an upper middle class of well-to-do merchants, and a lower middle class of artisans and small shopkeepers. The unpropertied urban proletariat did not function as an effective political class after the Jacquerie uprisings in the fourteenth century. Renaissance rationality demanded that the new patterns of urban power find expression in urban form. Whereas the ideal urban projects of Brunelleschi, Alberti, and Leonardo da Vinci were frustrated by town interests still powerful enough to resist ruthless demolition and vast breaches in the tightly knit urban fabric of Florence and Rome, such schemes could become a practical reality in the Paris of Henry IV.[25]

The three famous urban projects conceived under Henry IV were consciously tailored to the new class pattern. The Place Royale (now the Place des Vosges), begun in 1605 as a square surrounded by uniform town houses of appreciable scale and a generous quantity of Renaissance décor, was intended as a fashionable residential location for the *haute bourgeoisie* and the *noblesse de robe* (*Figs. 43–44*). The Place Dauphine, begun in 1607, was triangular in shape to conform with its site at the western tip of the Ile de la Cité and was a step down the social ladder (*Figs. 19, 35, 46*). The houses were smaller, included shops on the ground floor, and stylistically expressed the social level of their tenants by exterior rustication without pilasters. The Place de France, designed in 1610, adjoined the northern town wall and was to be a semicircular marketplace surrounded by large buildings, intended for public services (*Figs. 45, 47*).[26] An outer concentric street and eight radial streets, named after and symbolizing the provinces, were to be flanked by uniform houses for artisans and shopkeepers. The artisans' houses were of unadorned simplicity, whereas the public buildings with their towers and corner turrets expressed by their deliberate archaism the low social level of the entire complex. Renaissance theorists of architecture (Alberti, Palladio, Serlio) demanded that mercantile structures of this kind were to be accorded no ennobling vestige of antique form.[27]

Henry IV's projects have received much attention and praise as early examples of town planning.[28] But some of the most instructive lessons to be learned from them have passed unremarked. It should be emphasized, for example, that the sites of these projects were not simply cut into the existing urban fabric. In fact, they involved no extensive demolition whatever. The Place Royale was built on the site of the former royal residence and jousting links, the Hôtel des Tournelles, which suddenly had become unpopular after Henry II was killed there in a tournament. The site, in turn, was part of the Marais, the swampy eastern end of town inside the wall of Charles V which had remained almost wholly unsettled. The Place de France was to be in the same area in the open field behind the great fortified enclosure built by the Templiers in the twelfth century (*Fig. 34*). As for the Place Dauphine, in the late fourteenth century the court had moved out of the old palace to the Bastille end of town, leaving the buildings on the island to the hereditary *parlement*. It must have seemed no more than common sense to the business-like Henry IV, his minister, the Duc de Sully, and the nominal owner of the property, the premier president of the *parlement*, Achille de Harlay, to transform the old *jardin royal* at the tip of the island into a combination commercial and residential quarter.

The formidable obstacles to sheer urban survival faced by these royal schemes have also escaped notice. The largest and most consciously upper class of the group, the Place Royale—conceived on a totally new scale, with a large interior open plaza representing unheard-of luxury in the consumption of public space—was not designed to contain any ground floor shops of the kind which gave the Place Dauphine a semicommercial quality that related it to the surrounding medieval town. The upper class tenants who inhabited this new fashionable setting on the edge of town were torn out of the immediate context of their daily business affairs in the inner city. Living in this new location implied a walk or a ride on horseback or in a carriage for the purpose of getting into the center of town: a new kind of problem. One must conclude that the Place Royale, far from being the fertilizing center of the new Marais quarter, was an oversized urban parasite clinging to the adjacent tightly knit and active medieval town. The city didn't need it; it needed the city.

For closely related reasons only a few limited features of the Place de France scheme ever emerged from the project stage. Whereas the other two developments met a genuine demand for a new kind of "class-conscious" housing, no pressing need existed in

Paris for a planned quarter of dwellings for the lower class of artisans and shopkeepers who found their natural locations scattered throughout the old streets of the medieval town. As for the large buildings for undefined public services, the as-yet-undeveloped area was not prepared to digest such an overdose of institutional buildings, nor could the cost of building the new radial streets be justified in terms of access to these isolated structures alone. Such streets had to await the natural growth of the quarter; they could not precede it.

In many ways the Place Dauphine was the most urban scheme of the three (*Figs. 19, 35, 46*). Relatively modest in scale and of mixed residential and commercial usage, it also had the advantage of a central location not far from the active quarters on either side of the Seine. This centrality, however, was more potential than real as long as the tip of the Ile de la Cité remained isolated from the opposite river banks. The key to the Place Dauphine was the new bridge running across the tip of the island; the idea of the Pont Neuf, in fact, preceded the Place Dauphine. Henry III had laid the first stone in 1578, but the bridge was left uncompleted during the Religious Wars (1562–1598). In 1598 Henry IV resumed its construction, following a revised, simpler design. The penetration of the Left Bank was accomplished with the new Rue Dauphine running straight out to the Porte de Bucy which, in turn, gave access to the still-isolated Bourg Saint-Germain-des-Prés and its flourishing market (*Figs. 37, 48*). This bridge and street were unquestionably Henry's most significant contribution to the urban growth of Paris. The Faubourg Saint-Germain was now open for development.

Not long afterward, during the minority of Louis XIII, the eastern end of the city received similar attention. Two barren islands in the Seine were joined to compose the Ile Saint-Louis (*Figs. 37, 43, 49*) and were developed by a company under the entrepreneur Christopher Marie. Laid out on a grid plan as the rationale of the site and its rapid exploitation demanded, the project allowed for no luxuries of open space. It compensated for the rigidity of its layout by not prescribing a uniform building design to prospective residents, so that buildings of varying scale from the great Hôtel de Bretonvilliers at the southeast to modest apartment houses with ground floor shops lined the narrow streets. Its isolation was broken by two new bridges, the Pont Marie and the Pont de la Tournelle.

During these years were also realized the best features of the Place de France project, namely a few of the originally planned radiating streets, reminiscent of the sixteenth-century pattern of streets emanating from the Piazza del Popolo in Rome. Completed around 1636, the main arteries, the Rue Charlot with its extension running south and the Rues de Poitou and d'Anjou extending due east and northwest, effectively covered the Marais quarter (*Fig. 47*). The most important street of this group, however, was the long Rue-Neuve Saint-Louis (now Rue de Turenne), which linked the new northeast quarter to the area around the Place Royale. It is notable that these streets were executed and that they continue to retain their importance despite the fact that their intended focal point, the Place de France, was never built. It was an experience that Haussmann was to repeat two hundred years later: As we have seen, some of his most important connecting streets have insignificant terminations at one or both ends.

From the days of the revolution of Étienne Marcel in 1358, the former splendid harmony between crown and the city had been broken. Charles V had moved out of the old royal residence on the Ile de la Cité, where he had barely escaped assassination during the uprising, and into the Hôtel St.-Pol near the Bastille. State functions were carried on in the protection of the Louvre fortress. By the end of the fifteenth century Charles V's successors were spending most of their time in their castles on the Loire. The urge to move out to the edge of town and beyond remained a persistent trait in the royal character. Urban interest and royal interest were no longer identical because the royal power was no longer based on the city alone. It relied instead on the resources of the entire nation, which was gradually united around and subordinated to the crown. This political mutation was bound to leave its mark on the city. As the conflict between town and crown became a struggle between two powers of unequal dimensions, the new urban patterns revealed striking contrasts of scale which the medieval city had never known. The planned schemes of Henry IV, with their rigid patterns and open spaces, reflect this change of scale. But the most significant expression of the new trend was the growth of the Louvre (*Figs. 35, 50–51*).

The idea of razing the old Louvre (*Fig. 34*) in order to begin a new royal palace in its place originated with Francis I. Execution of the project began in the 1550's under his successor, Henry II, and Henry's architect Pierre Lescot.[29] In the form it eventually attained under Louis XIV and Louis XV, including the Palais des Tuileries and its great garden, it represented a vast obstacle to the organic westward growth of the city between the river and the Rue St.-Honoré. One is tempted today to think that the Louvre has always existed more or less in its final form, that given it by Napoleon III: a great blocklike complex extending from the colonnaded eastern façade opposite St.-Germain-l'Auxerrois to the Palais des Tuileries nearly half a mile to the west, with the garden stretching on to the Place de la Concorde beyond. But the growth of the Louvre was not an unobstructed triumphal march of royal power over prostrate urban interests. Its three-century-long agony of expansion is an instructive lesson in urban politics.

The failure to realize great architectural conceptions is sometimes attributed regretfully to a combination of infirmity of purpose and purse and the shortsighted opposition of special interest groups. In the case of the Louvre we must consider it a result of urban self-defense. The protective mechanism consisted quite simply of encroachment: The expanding Louvre ran into formidable obstacles (*Fig. 50*). In the late thirteenth and early fourteenth centuries a *faubourg* had grown up around the old fortress outside the Porte Saint-Honoré, its regular blocks indicating rapid development. At the *faubourg's* outer limit, where it eventually became encircled by the new wall of Charles V, Saint Louis had founded the Hospice des Quinze-Vingts for blind beggars. One institution was thus pushing against another, and the hospital with its *faubourg* had evident powers of resistance: In fact, the building and its surrounding quarters survived into the middle of the nineteenth century. Whatever the ambitions of Francis I and his successors, the Louvre found itself pressed against the river, attempting to outflank the apparently immovable obstacles to its growth. The most important building of this early phase, the Palais des Tuileries (1563–1594), built for the queen mother, Catherine de Medicis, was outside the wall of Charles V in open country, where it encroached on and was, in turn, encroached upon by the ever-growing Faubourg Saint-Honoré. In the end, the case of the Louvre *vs.* Paris must be considered a standoff. The irresistible force and the immovable object gradually came to terms with each other.

What the previous kings had not managed to do was accomplished by Louis XIII's minister: It was the Cardinal Richelieu who built the first genuinely royal town residence in the growing west end of the city. Marie de Medicis had made a bold attempt in her residence, the Palais du Luxembourg (begun in 1615), but despite all its scale and splendor it was at the southern end of town, outside the walls (*Fig. 52*). The Palais-Cardinal (built in 1632, renamed the Palais-Royal in 1642, and extensively rebuilt in the eighteenth century) extended boldly northward from the Rue St.-Honoré across the confines of the wall of Charles V, which Richelieu partly demolished, and had truly royal scale. The young Louis XIV was glad that his father's old minister had left it to the crown upon his death in 1642. When he acceded to the throne a year later he moved in with his mother, Anne of Austria, the regent, and lived in it as long as he remained in Paris. His first minister, the Cardinal Mazarin, favorite of the queen mother, established himself directly behind the new Palais-Royal. (*Fig. 63*). The Rue de Richelieu (*Fig. 50*) opened up the virgin area newly enclosed by the wall extension (known as the *enceinte* of Louis XIII) which brought the town limits to the western end of the Jardins des Tuileries (*Fig. 35*). Extending across the western end of the city like a great exclamation point, the Palais-Royal was no less an obstruction to the organic growth of the quarter than the Louvre.

Whereas French efforts to secure a foothold in the East Indies met with limited success in the face of Dutch and English competition, Champlain's explorations in North America and the founding of Quebec in 1609 laid potentially profitable colonies at the country's feet. For at least a century the French also had important trading interests in India. Richelieu's astute European policy during the Thirty Years War (1618–1648) brought the country out of that conflict as the chief power in Europe.

The pace and extent of international commercial and scientific life was increasing rapidly, and urban scale was bound to change with it. Richelieu did more than build a palace fit for a king. Following the course established two decades before by Henry IV, he set the country and the city of Paris firmly on the course it was to steer for the next hundred years. When the old public hospital on the Ile de la Cité, the Hôtel Dieu, had become insufficient for the needs of the growing city during the plague of 1606, Henry IV had responded with the great pest hospital of Saint-Louis, outside the Porte du Temple (*Figs. 19, 53–54*). Richelieu rebuilt the Sorbonne and included a monumental chapel (1624–1642; *Fig. 55*). In 1641, Louis XIII founded the royal herb garden, ancestor of the later Jardin des Plantes outside of town along the banks of the Seine and the Bièvre rivers behind the Abbaye St.-Victor (*Fig. 56*). Mazarin donated his library and funds for a new institution for boys from the newly acquired provinces, the Collège des Quatre-Nations. Finally built in the 1660's, it found its place on the site of the old Tour de Nesle, the last surviving fragment of Philip Augustus' wall on the Left Bank, opposite the Louvre.

The need for ever-more-specialized facilities for medical treatment was met with the transformation of an old arsenal beyond the Jardin des Plantes, the Salpêtrière, into a hospital for the mentally ill (1656; *Fig. 57*). Monastic foundations also became oversized. In 1638, Anne of Austria, overjoyed at the birth of Louis XIV, gave Paris a complex on its southern fringe to compete with the Escorial and St. Peter's: the church and abbey of Val-de-Grâce (*Fig. 58*).

Colbert, advisor to Louis XIV, maintained the trend toward continuously larger institutional scale. Hoping to keep Louis XIV in Paris, he concentrated his architectural efforts on the completion of the Louvre.[30] But Louis was not to be molded by Colbert. Breaking the tradition of urban residence established by Henry IV, he left for Versailles (*Fig. 59*). Colbert created the first industrial suburb of Paris by organizing the Flemish Gobelin weavers, long settled on the banks of the Bièvre outside of town, into the Mobilier National. The Observatoire (1667–1672) behind the Couvent des Chartreux (destroyed in 1798) became the city's first establishment for scientific research (*Figs. 60–61*).[31] When the gigantic Hôtel des Invalides (1671–1676), a home for the old and wounded veterans of Louis' unceasing wars, was finally complete with Jules Hardouin-Mansart's immense chapel of St.-Louis (1679–1708) tacked on in back, Paris was literally surrounded by great Baroque edifices (*Figs. 18, 62*). The question is whether they served or strangled the growing city.

Francis I's decision to rehabilitate the old Louvre on the western edge of the city had historic consequences. The town could neither fight nor ignore the royal resident in whose hands the reins of national wealth and power were ever more firmly held. Slowly but steadily the urban center of gravity moved away from the Ile de la Cité and the Right Bank, drawn as if by a magnet to the new pole of political power on the edge of the city.

The Pont Neuf (1578–1606) had, as we have seen, opened up the Faubourg Saint-Germain (*Fig. 19*). The demolition of Charles V's wall and the building of the Rue de Richelieu (*Fig. 63*) had cleared the way for the development of the Faubourg Saint-Honoré. By the end of the seventeenth century both *faubourgs* had become the fashionable places of residence for the *haute bourgeoisie* and the town nobility. The gradual progress in this development can be traced in the history of the Pont Royal, which crossed the river just east of the Palais des Tuileries. In the 1550's Henry II had authorized a ferry service which has left its trace in the Rue du Bac (meaning ferry) on the Left Bank. A wooden bridge was built in 1632, abutting the Rue de Beaune on the south side. Burned in 1656, it was replaced by another wooden bridge. When the second bridge was swept away in a flood in 1684, Louis XIV decided on the construction of the still-surviving stone bridge (1685–1689). The west end of the city had become the new center of Paris.

This development was celebrated and accelerated by two urban projects of Louis XIV's later years, both carried out by the ubiquitous Hardouin-Mansart. The first, the circular Place des Victoires, projected in 1685, was more than "a piece of exaggerated flattery to the King."[32] From this the focal point of the fast-growing financial and business center developing behind the Palais-Royal radiated both new and old roads (*Fig. 64*). The Rue Croix des Petits-Champs, once just outside the wall of Philip Augustus, connected the Place des Victoires with the Louvre, while two new streets (the present Rue du Mail, Rue de Cléry, and Rue d'Aboukir), following the line of the old rampart and moat of Charles V, joined it to the Porte Saint-Denis (rebuilt in 1672). The latter streets must be considered an integral and essential part of the scheme, as was the Rue-Neuve des Petits-Champs running due west of the Place, parallel to the Rue du Faubourg Saint-Honoré and between the Palais-Royal and the Palais Mazarin. The Palais Mazarin (1645) was soon to house the royal library and the Bourse, the new center of commerce. The length of these streets, their focus on the gilt statue of Louis XIV in the center of the Place des Victoires, as well as the unified monumental elevations around the Place are an indication not merely of the absolutist pretensions of the king but also of the new spirit of "big business."

Louis XIV's second project, the new Place Royale (now the Place Vendôme), gave an even more impressive focus to the quarter farther west and merits similar consideration (*Figs. 50, 65*). It was symptomatic of the predominance of urban over institutional interests that Louis XIV's plan to surround the new Place with the royal library and the academies came to nought, and that the Place became another center of upper class residence. There seems to be little point in comparing the new Place Royale with the old one of Henry IV and of lamenting that the houses were "handed over not to the useful citizens who inhabited the [old] Place Royale but to the excessively wealthy and somewhat ostentatious financiers who built their hotels around it."[33] The scale of both business and architecture and the image building of financial tycoons had changed since the days of Henry IV.

Our comments concerning the plazas of Henry IV (pp. 34–36) apply to these Baroque projects as well. Both were built in previously open areas. Both initially led a semiparasitic existence, taking more than they were giving. The Place des Victoires was in close contact with the active commercial quarter around St.-Eustache and Les Halles in the western corner of the old city of Philip Augustus. The new Place Royale drew its urban sustenance from the developed, lively Rue du Faubourg Saint-Honoré. Again, the streets relating to the plazas were probably more significant from an urban point of view than the plazas themselves (*Fig. 18*).

The progressive alteration of the buildings facing onto the Place des Victoires demonstrates how a living urban environment will shape the most intractable abstraction into usable form. That the Place Vendôme has not endured a similar transformation is probably because the motley and varied buildings which arose behind its uniform façades lent themselves more readily to a gradual adaptation that could proceed without touching the façades in front. Great plans and institutions come and go, but the buildings remain, and cities have to live with or replace them.

While the age of Louis XIV could not eliminate the dense quarter pressing against the Louvre, it developed the area west of the Tuileries palace with a great display of Baroque garden design. Marie de Medicis had created a fashionable tree-lined promenade along the river, the Cours-la-Reine, west of the Jardins des Tuileries. In the 1660's Louis XIV's garden architect, André Le Nôtre (1613–1700), began the redevelopment of the palace gardens. Up to its western limits at the later Place de la Concorde it was a tailored display of geometrical beds and arbors. From here on a great axial road lined with large trees ran westward through the orderly tree aisles of the Champs Elysées toward a first circular plaza with radiating avenues, the present Rond Point (*Fig. 66*). In the early eighteenth century the scheme was extended outward to the crest of the Chaillot hill, terminating in a second larger circular plaza, the Place de l'Étoile. The still less formal Bois de Boulogne to the west, transversed by long diagonal roads, marks a third stage in the orderly transition from cultured garden to open country reminiscent of the large-scaled sense of order and rationality of the *Grande Siècle*.

A growing Paris was being surrounded by institutional blocks set into open spaces which could not be other than vast breaks in the expanding urban fabric. With the spreading Faubourg Saint-Germain already bounded on the west by the Invalides, Louis XV added another supersized obstacle to future growth westward when he founded the École Militaire on the Plaine de Grenelle in 1751. Its huge drill field, the Champ-de-Mars, extended northwest to the Seine (*Figs. 18, 67*).

The king's name graced the last of the great royal squares in Paris, Jacques-Ange Gabriel's masterpiece: the Place Louis XV (1757–1772, now the Place de la Concorde; *Figs. 18, 68–71*). The project was financed by the city on land partially donated by the king. Both crown and city had to be served, and they were served in proportion to the existing balance of power. The Place cannot and should not be evaluated in isolation from the urban context. It was part of a coherent project that extended from the river to the church of Ste.-Madeleine (which replaced an older parish chapel nearby) and comprised three new streets connecting the Place with the Rue du Faubourg Saint-Honoré: the axial Rue Royale, projected as early as 1732, and two lesser parallel streets to either side, the Rue Champs-Elysées (now the Rue Boissy d'Anglais) and the Rue St.-Florentin. The scheme had two focal points, the Place Louis XV and the Place de la Madeleine; a connecting axis, the Rue Royale; and a major intersection at the crossing of the Rue Royale and the Rue du Faubourg Saint-Honoré.

The Place Louis XV was not intended to be an urban space, but rather was designed to mark a graceful transition between two units of a great Baroque east-west palace axis: the manicured palace gardens of the Tuileries and the ordered but less cultivated promenade parks of the Champs-Elysées and the old Cours-la-Reine (1616) of Marie de Médicis along the river. Toward the Rue Royale the Place figured as an intermediate area between the public and penetrable urban quarter created around the new streets and the impenetrable private area of the palace grounds. The city begins— or ends, as it were—with two monumental palaces facing the square on the north. The intended isolation of the Place from its adjacent urban environment was originally emphasized by deep dry moats which turned the central area into an island made accessible by four bridges. But with the statue of Louis XV on horseback preempting the center, the little sentry-box-like stair towers in the eight corners complicating the outline, and the surrounding buildings failing to clarify it, the Place was literally not a "place," its outline intentionally undefined, its edges fluid.

By contrast the Rue Royale and its flanking streets, for all their formality, presented a genuinely urban environment of shops and residences. When the Pont de la Concorde (1787-1791) was finally completed with stones from the Bastille in the last year of Louis XVI's reign, the increasingly lively western quarters on each side of the river were in direct connection. Nothing, however, could overcome the inherent antiurban characteristics of the Place Louis XV. Its new name of 1792, Place de la Révolution, and its guillotine came and went (*Fig. 70*); the great space became the Place de la Concorde in 1795. Napoleon I turned the projected Madeleine into a temple; an obelisk from Luxor took the place of the equestrian royal statue. During the July Monarchy J.-I. Hittorf added fountains and sculpture and filled in the surrounding moats. But the space only became even bigger and less definable. A masterpiece of rococo design, it was from the beginning and remains to this day an enormous traffic circle. Although the Rue Royale and its subsidiary streets were a concession to genuine urban needs, they were but limited compensation for such a vast and intractable break in the fabric of the city's fastest-growing area. The Place held up the active urban development of the quarter between the river and the Champs-Elysées for nearly a century: a high price to pay for a *pièce de résistance*.

The only major construction of lasting urban significance from the years following the Revolution was the transformation of the Palais Bourbon into the site of the first legislative chamber of the new republic in 1795. The new Pont de la Concorde formed its access to the center of town on the Right Bank (*Fig. 72*).

Napoleon I (*Fig. 73*), for all his grandiose intentions, had little time left over for turning Paris into the ideal city of his Empire. Aside from his triumphal arches and columns, the transformation of the Madeleine into an imperial temple (1806; *Fig. 74*), the establishment of the École Polytechnique (1805) in the old Collège de Navarre (founded 1304), and the improvement of the water supply via the Canal de l'Ourc (1802; *Fig. 59*), Napoleon's main urban effort was the Rue de Rivoli (1811), a semiresidential, semicommercial street with arcaded ground floors, linking the Louvre and the inner city with the Place de la Concorde (*Fig. 72*). The Rue de Castiglione branched off to join the Rue de Rivoli with the Place Vendôme while the new Rue des Pyramides, further east, provided another connection with the Rue-Neuve des Petits-Champs. Important as these new streets are, they were not a major contribution.

The Arc de Triomphe (1806–1836), finished long after Napoleon's death, beckoned Parisians out to the far end of the Champs-Elysées, but its Place de l'Étoile, on the edge of the wall built with Ledoux's *barrières* in the 1780's (*Fig. 75*), had to await Haussmann and the middle of the nineteenth century for incorporation into the growing city (*Fig. 76*).

Little was done during the Restoration, the Bourbons having, as the saying went, "learnt nothing and forgotten nothing." Louis Philippe and his Parisian prefect, the Count de Rambuteau, began to provide the prisons, hospitals, asylums, schools, libraries, and a few of the streets which the new middle class society required. The Hôtel de Ville was restructured to nineteenth-century scale (1837–1849), receiving new wings to contain the growing city administration while retaining its sixteenth-century core. Some of the outer boulevards were paved and planted with trees. The first omnibus transportation was introduced. Even more important, Louis Philippe supported the development of interurban railways and saw the completion of the first railroad terminals (*Figs. 8–9*). Significantly, the railroads terminated at the edge of the then-existing city. No one dreamed of cutting a passage for these iron roads into the heart of the city. The problems the terminals presented—the smoke, soot, smells, and sudden explosions of travelers pressing into the city from each arriving train—were left to resolve themselves in the open fields at the edge of town. It is an aspect of railroad planning one is apt to forget today when the terminals have long been engulfed by the expanding city.

Then appeared Napoleon III and his Prefect of the Seine.

CRITICAL EVALUATION: 2

Paris as a city evolved from the effective collaboration of urban commercial interests and an increasingly centralized state. Problems as well as opportunities were created by the various and large-scale additions to the medieval city. We have already discussed the effects of the bourgeois revolution, its industrial counterpart, and the resulting massive increase in urban population. All observers agree that by 1850 Paris was no longer suited to the changed conditions and that a concerted attack on its manifold problems was imperative (*Fig. 77*). We have already outlined the nature of the program of Napoleon III and Haussmann and the evaluations of some of its major critics. All agree that a great effort was made, but they disagree as to the extent to which it was an urban, aesthetic, and social success.

There can be no disagreement as to the importance of the large-scale sewer, water, and street-lighting systems built during the Second Empire. From any point of view, these systems were basic for all else. Beyond this the consensus ends. Some critics like the new streets, some the parks and the new buildings, others reject individual aspects or the whole of the Haussmann project as either aesthetically unsatisfying or socially inadequate.

Some significant points appear to have been overlooked. Regardless of whether one considers mid-nineteenth-century lower class housing in Paris adequate or inadequate—and the compulsion to impose their ideas of what are or are not adequate living conditions has been one of the cardinal weaknesses of many twentieth-century urban planners—the lower classes were in one way or another served by the existing city of 1850. Masses of them lived, worked, played, and died within the old city which had been their habitat for centuries. If there was anything wrong with the old city, it was that there was not enough of it for the skyrocketing population. But to a degree that problem was solving itself in the way it always had: The latest comers simply had to take their place at the burgeoning periphery. By the 1850's, in fact, the mass of newcomers had spread out beyond the eighteenth-century limits, settling in and around the outlying villages included within the new ring of fortifications put up by the July Monarchy in the 1840's (*Fig. 59*). Freshly off the farm with its drudgery and declining income, the new arrivals saw in the city not a prison of industrial slavery but the promise of a rising standard of living. The crowded conditions, sordid smells, rampant epidemics, high prices, lack of adequate public transport, physical insecurity, and sheer filth of the city posed only limited terrors to a group which had left little to regret behind them. They had only one overriding fear that could move them to violent action: unemployment.

But the urban middle class, and the rising upper middle class in particular, were not so well served by the existing city. There had always been housing of one kind or another for the very poor of Paris, and palaces for the very rich. But aside from the squares of Henry IV and Louis XIV and the Ile Saint-Louis, the Rue Royale, the Rue de Rivoli, and the outer ring of boulevards cleared by Louis XIV (*Fig. 78*), there was not much of a residential environment suitable for the middle and upper class bourgeois. Yet it was precisely this urban middle class that had fomented and dominated the revolution and which, after the ups and downs of the first half of the century, was now firmly in the political saddle. The empire of Napoleon III was its political tool, and the middle class was determined to use it. Internal political conflicts of the Second Empire were not so much between the upper and lower urban classes as between the urban bourgeoisie of Paris and the *petite bourgeoisie* of the provinces. The lower class in the city could be controlled by the police and pacified with employment opportunities in massive construction projects. But the bourgeois of the provinces could only see Paris as a glittering magnet that attracted the working population out of the countryside and led to higher prices, as a dangerous distraction which kept the government from looking after the interests of the rest of the country.

To see the kind of city which the rising Parisian upper middle class wanted and demanded and which the Paris of 1850 provided not at all or in insufficient degree, we have only to sketch out the kind of life which was both their ideal and, due to the increasing funds at the disposal of a growing number of people, an incipient reality. Our typical upper middle class man-in-the-street is self-made, having risen from peddling to riches by that most promising of routes, merchandising on a new scale and for a new scale of population, with goods put at his disposal by the mass-producing machine. In short, he owns a department store (*Figs. 79–80*). He increases his wealth by speculation in stocks and real estate in a rising market. He becomes a financier, makes daring investments. His political connections are firm. Commercial travel holds no terrors for him. He travels by train, first class, demands a new class of hotels near the railway stations of the towns he visits, and develops expensive tastes in restaurants, theaters, vacation resorts, and women (*Fig. 81*).

Returning to Paris he wants a direct and prestigious route to his home from the station (*Fig. 17*). Home can no longer be the modest side-street apartment of former years nor—for he is not that rich—a *hôtel particulier* in the old quarters of the faded aristocracy. Home is exactly what and where he wants it to be: an elegant, plushly furnished apartment on one of the lower floors of the new apartment houses lining the boulevards, which are snapped up as soon as they are built (*Figs. 32, 82*). Flush toilets and hot and cold running water grace his bathroom. He has gas lighting and steam heat, of course.

The old class of retail stores and restaurants no longer meets his requirements in clothing, food, and luxuries. A new class of establishments to purvey these items finds its place on the lower floors of the new boulevard houses (*Fig. 83*). Having greeted his wife with a kiss he takes her—or perhaps his mistress—to an evening of relaxation at the new opera house (*Fig. 84*)—that most nineteenth century of places—and to a late supper at a high-class restaurant afterward (*Fig. 85*). On Sunday he is off, this time definitely with his wife and children, to absorb culture at the Louvre museum. After that a carriage ride to the Bois de Boulogne to enjoy the spectacle of the artificial waterfall in action—a daily afternoon sensation—then perhaps an hour at the Longchamps races.

He was a busy man, but connections were fast. In no time at all one could look after one's interests at the Bourse, litigate at the Tribunal de Commerce, or serve justice at the criminal courts, the last two now conveniently concentrated on the Cité, and get back to one's business in town. The bureaucracy in its numerous and spacious ministries was plodding but efficient, the University large and secular. The Académie des Beaux-Arts and the Conservatoire de Musique were turning out respectable artists *en masse* to fulfill the demands for art, architecture, and music. The cabarets (*Fig. 86*) were gay and the newspapers sensational. It was indeed the best of all possible worlds, and Napoleon and Haussmann were bringing it about.

When the Second Empire fell under the weight of its own pretensions and the onslaught of the newly powerful and ruthlessly efficient German military machine, Haussmann had already been forced from the scene by political pressures, but his work was nearly complete and his successors in the Third Republic could not but finish it for him. Critics tend to claim that the bourgeoisie resisted Haussmann's efforts every step of the way and finally overthrew him. This view is not supported by the political facts. Any large-scale urban alterations will favor certain interests, damage others, and arouse some noisy opposition. Conservatives in banking, industry, and

1. Napoleon III (left) and Baron Georges-Eugène Haussmann (right) discussing plans for the transformation of Paris. (Bibliothèque Historique de la Ville de Paris.)

2. German troops entering Paris, 1870. (Engraving by Julius Ehrentraut in the *Illustrierte Zeitung für Volk und Heer.*)

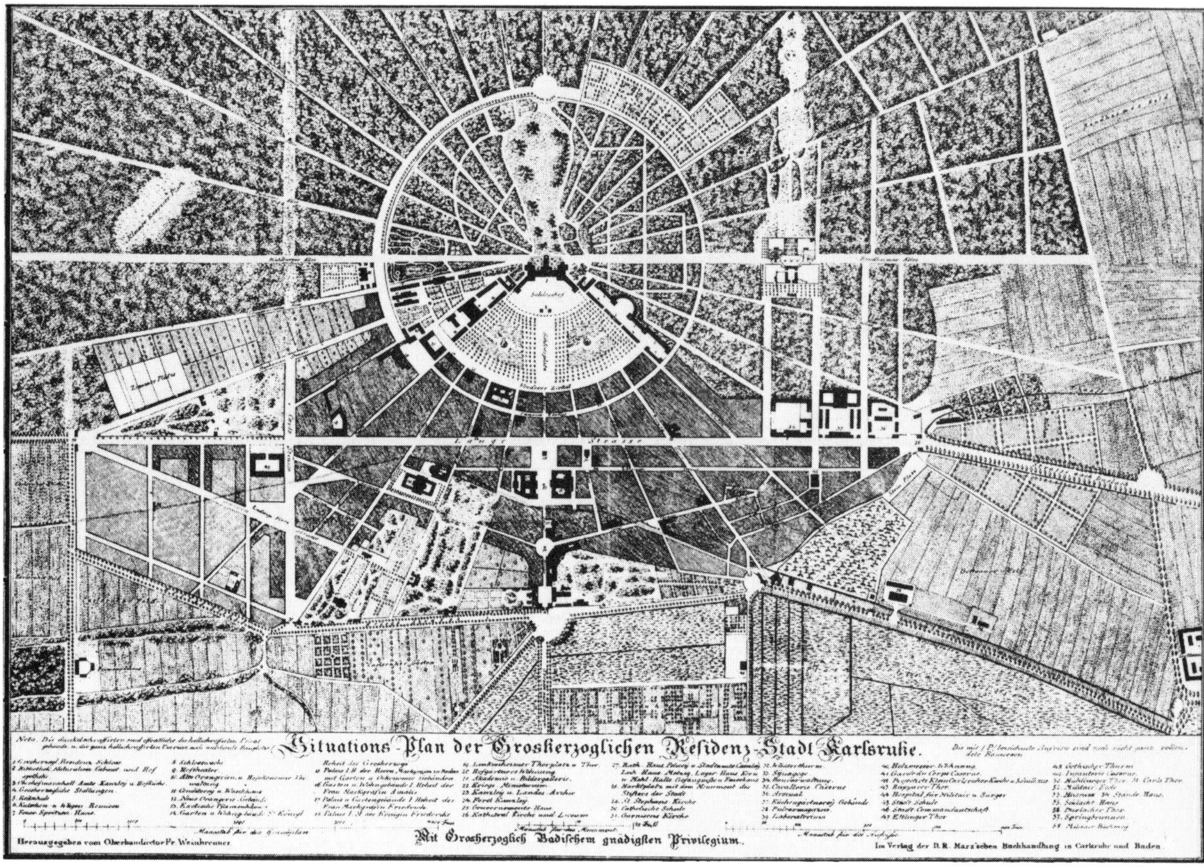

3. Karlsruhe, plan of 1822.

4. Karlsruhe, Rondellplatz with Ettlingertor (demolished). Small scale is characteristic of the ideal city of the bourgeois revolution.

5. Claude-Nicolas Ledoux: Ideal city of Chaux, perspective view. Saltworks are in the center, ringed by residential buildings with gardens. Outside are the various communal facilities. (From Ledoux, *L'Architecture considerée sous le rapport de l'art, des moeurs et de la legislation* [1804].)

6. Claude-Nicolas Ledoux: Cannon foundry near Chaux. (From Ledoux, *L'Architecture considerée sous le rapport de l'art, des moeurs et de la legislation* [1804].)

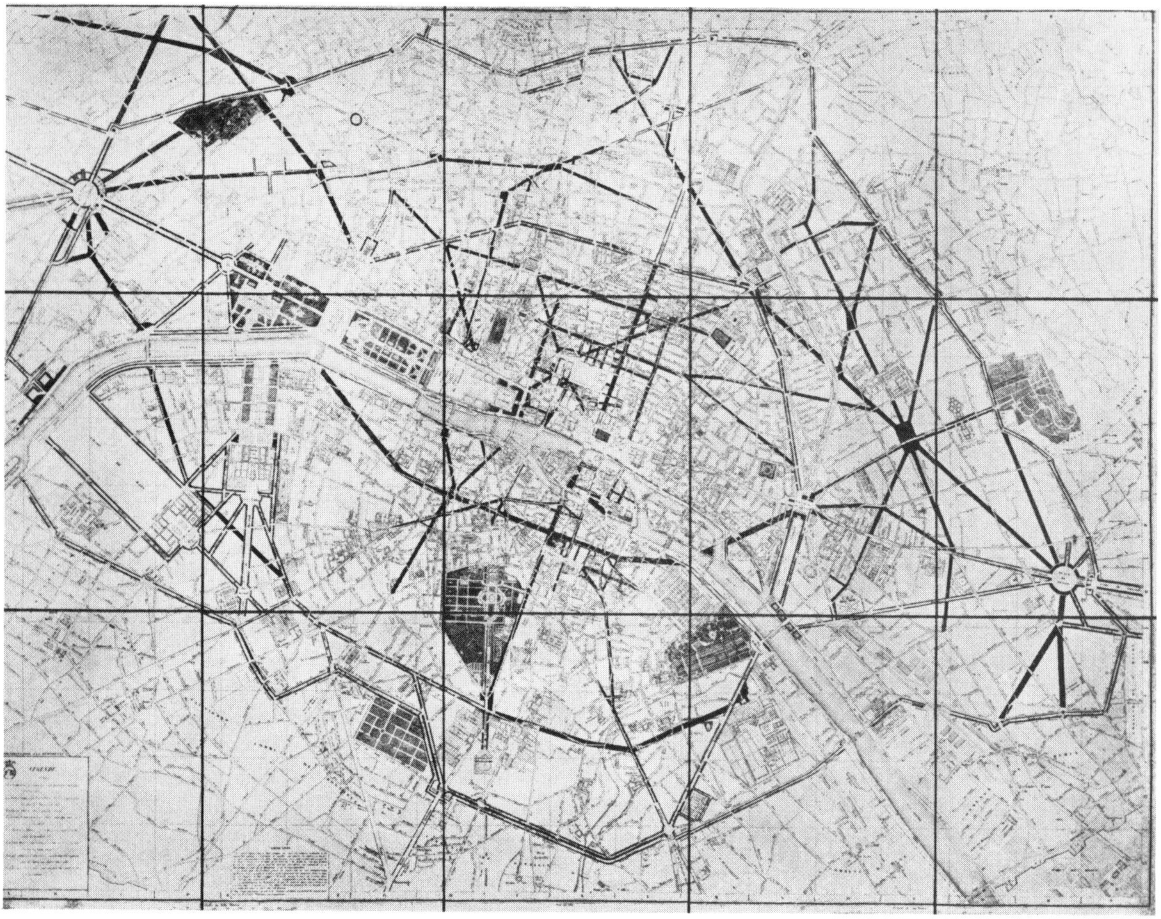

7. Map of Paris by Napoleon III, c. 1852. Dark lines mark proposed new boulevards.

8. Tunnel, Gare St. Lazare. Station platform is at right. (From Texier, *Tableau de Paris* [1852].)

9. Strasbourg railway terminal in Paris (now Gare de l'Est). Above, front. Below, rear. (From Texier.)

10. Fighting in Rue St.-Antoine during the revolution of 1848. (Bibliothèque Nationale.)

11. Napoleon III, c. 1850. (Photo by Nadar.)

12. View of Paris looking northwest from the bell tower of St. Louis-en-Île, 1852. Hôtel de Ville is to right of bell tower. (From Texier.)

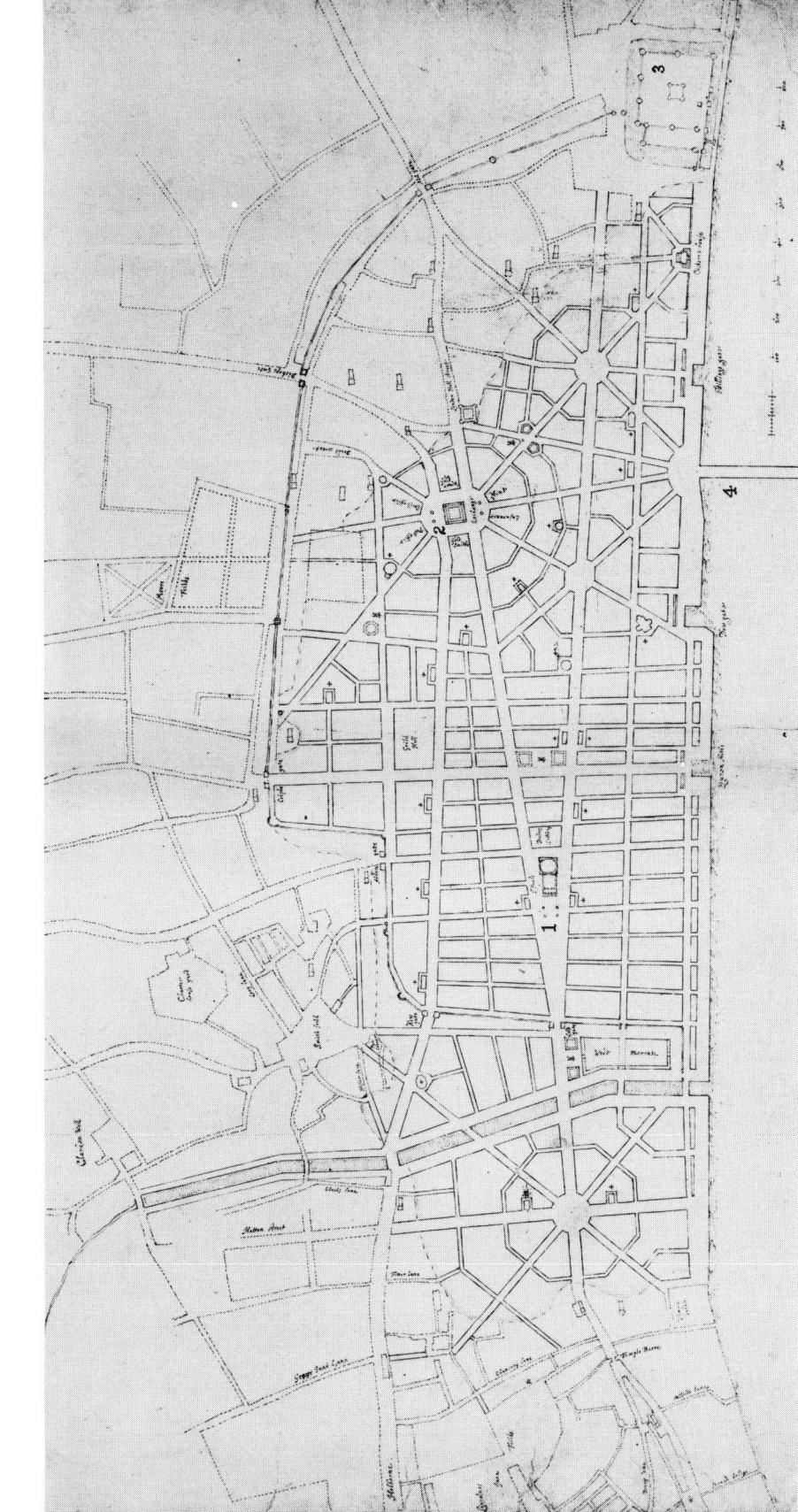

13. Christopher Wren: Plan for rebuilding London after the fire, 1666. Scale is in yards: (1) St. Paul's Cathedral, (2) Royal Exchange, (3) Tower, (4) London Bridge.

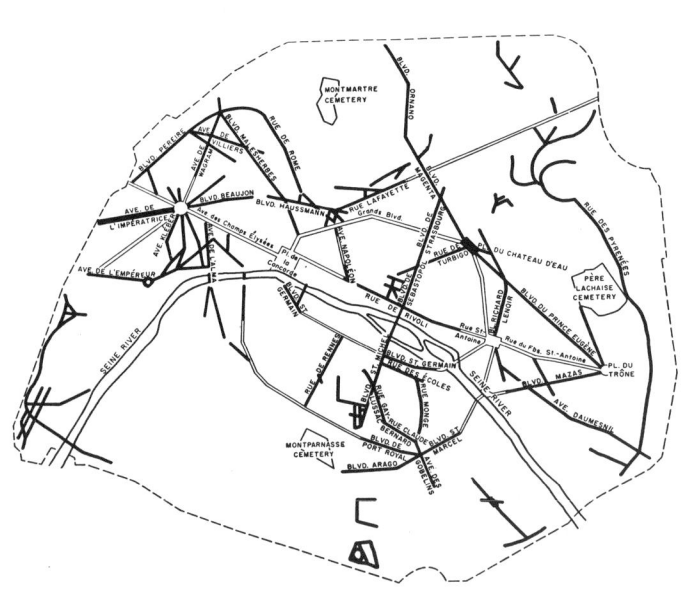

14. Rue de Rambuteau, seen from Boulevard Sébastopol, 1968.

15. Principal streets built from 1850 to 1870, Paris. (Based on Departement de la Seine, *Les Travaux de Paris, 1789–1889; Atlas* [Paris, 1889], plates XI and XII.)

16. Avenue de l'Opéra, c. 1880, looking toward the Louvre.

17. Boulevard, Paris, 1902.

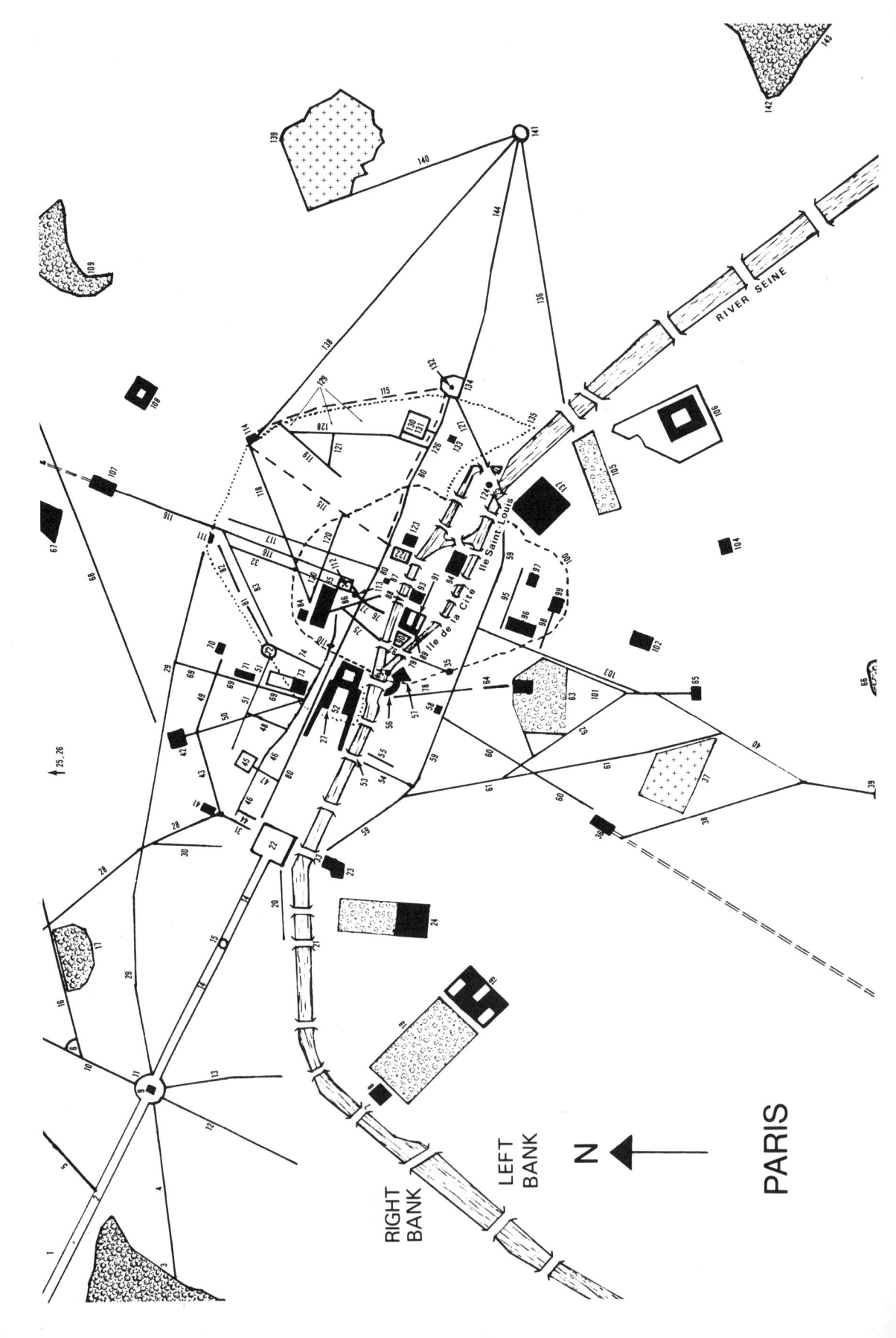

1. Neuilly
2. Av. de la Grand Armée
3. Bois de Boulogne
4. Av. Foch (formerly Av. de l'Imperatrice)
5. Blvd. Pereire
6. Pl. des Ternes
7. Pont d'Iéna
8. Eiffel Tower
9. Arc de Triomphe
10. Av. Wagram
11. Pl. de l'Étoile (Pl. de Charles de Gaulle)
12. Av. Kléber
13. Av. Marceau
14. Av. des Champs-Elysées
15. Rond Point
16. R. de Courcelles
17. Parc Monceau
18. Champ-de-Mars
19. École Militaire
20. Cours-la-Reine
21. Pont des Invalides
22. Pl. de la Concorde
23. Palais Bourbon (Nat. Assembly)
24. Hôtel des Invalides
25. Les Batignolles
26. Cim. Montmartre
27. Site: Hospice des Quinze-Vingts
28. Blvd. Malesherbes
29. Blvd. Haussmann
30. R. d'Anjou
31. R. Royale
32. R. St.-Denis
33. Pont de la Concorde
34. Site: Tour de Nesle
35. Site: Porte de Buci
36. Gare de Montparnasse
37. Cim. Montparnasse
38. Av. du Maine
39. Porte d'Orléans
40. Av. d'Orléans
41. La Madeleine
42. L'Opéra
43. Blvd. de la Madeleine
44. R. St.-Florentin
45. Pl. Vendôme
46. R. St.-Honoré
47. R. Castiglione
48. R. des Pyramides
49. R. du 4 Septembre
50. Av. de l'Opéra (formerly Av. Napoleon III)
51. R. des Petits-Champs
52. Louvre
53. Pont Royal
54. R. du Bac
55. R. de Beaune
56. Inst. de France
57. Hôtel des Monnaies
58. St.-Germain-des-Prés
59. Blvd. St.-Germain
60. R. de Rennes
61. Blvd. Raspail
62. R. d'Assas
63. Jardin & Palais du Luxembourg
64. R. Tournon
65. Observatoire
66. Parc de Montsouris
67. Gare du Nord
68. R. Lafayette
69. R. de Richelieu
70. Bourse
71. Bibl. Nat. (incorp. Palais Mazarin)
72. Pl. des Victoires
73. Palais-Royal
74. R. Croix des Petits-Champs
75. R. du Pont Neuf
76. R. des Lavandières
77. R. Ste. Opportune
78. R. de Seine
79. R. Dauphine
80. Rue de Rivoli
81. R. du Mail
82. Rue de Clery
83. R. d'Aboukir
84. St.-Eustache
85. Les Halles
86. R. des Halles
87. Tour St.-Jacques
88. Pont-au-Change
89. Palais de Justice
90. Pl. Dauphine
91. Ste.-Chapelle
92. Pont Neuf
93. Trib. de Commerce
94. Notre Dame
95. R. des Écoles
96. Sorbonne
97. École Polytéchnique
98. R. Soufflot
99. Panthéon (Ste.-Geneviève)
100. Site: Wall of Philip Augustus
101. Site: Couvent des Chartreux
102. Val-de-Grâce
103. Blvd. St.-Michel
104. Gobelins Factory
105. Jardin des Plantes
106. Hôspital Salpêtrière
107. Gare de l'Est
108. Hôpital Saint-Louis
109. Parc des Buttes Chaumont
110. Site of Porte Saint-Honoré
111. Porte Saint-Denis
112. Cimetière des Saints-Innocents
113. Site: Cloister of Saint Opportune
114. Site: Porte du Temple
115. Boundary: the Marais in 16th & 17th cents.
116. Blvd. Sébastopol
117. R. St.-Martin
118. R. de Turbigo
119. R. Charlot
120. R. de Rambuteau
121. R. de Poitou
122. Pl. de Grève
123. Hôtel de Ville
124. Site: Hôtel de Brétonvilliers
125. Pont Sully
126. R. St.-Antoine
127. Blvd. Henri IV
128. R. de Turenne
129. Site: Proposed Place de France
130. Place Royale (des Vosges)
131. Site: Hôtel de Tournelles
132. Colonne de la Bastille
133. Site: Hôtel St.-Pol
134. Site: Porte St.-Antoine
135. Site: Wall of Charles V
136. Blvd. Diderot
137. Halle aux Vins (site: Abbaye St.-Victor)
138. Blvd. Voltaire
139. Cimetière Père-Lachaise
140. Av. Philippe Auguste
141. Pl. de la Nation
142. Bois de Vincennes
143. Plateau de Gravelle
144. R. du Faubourg Saint-Antoine

19. Ile de la Cité, detail from Turgot plan of 1734. Note Pont Neuf, Palais-Royal, and Place Dauphine in foreground. Old Hôtel Dieu is in front of Notre Dame Cathedral and is linked by Petit Pont to Petit Chatelet.

20. Ile de la Cité from the air, with Ile Saint-Louis beyond, looking southeast. Palais de Justice (in foreground behind Place Dauphine) is an enlargement of the former palace complex. Note the Ste.-Chapelle, remaining in center courtyard. In the middle ground are the Tribunal de Commerce (left, its dome on axis with the Boulevard Sébastopol) and the Prefecture du Police (right). Beyond is Notre Dame Cathedral with its Place du Parvis. From rear to front, bridges linking islands with Right Bank are Pont Marie, Pont Louis-Philippe, Pont d'Arcole (leading to Hôtel de Ville), Pont Notre-Dame, and Pont-au-Change. From rear to front, bridges to Left Bank are Pont Sully, Pont de la Tournelle, Pont d'Archevêche, Pont au Double, Petit Pont, and Pont St.-Michel.

21. H. M. Lefuel: Pavilion Richelieu, Palais du Louvre, 1852–1857.

22. Victor Baltard: Les Halles (central markets), 1853, project. (From Baltard and Felix Callet, *Monographie des Halles Centrales* [Paris, 1863], plate I.)

23. Bois de Boulogne as transformed by Adolphe Alphand in the 1850's. (From Alphand, *Les Promenades de Paris* [Paris, 1867–1873].)

24. Bois de Boulogne, the Mare d'Auteuil, c. 1870.

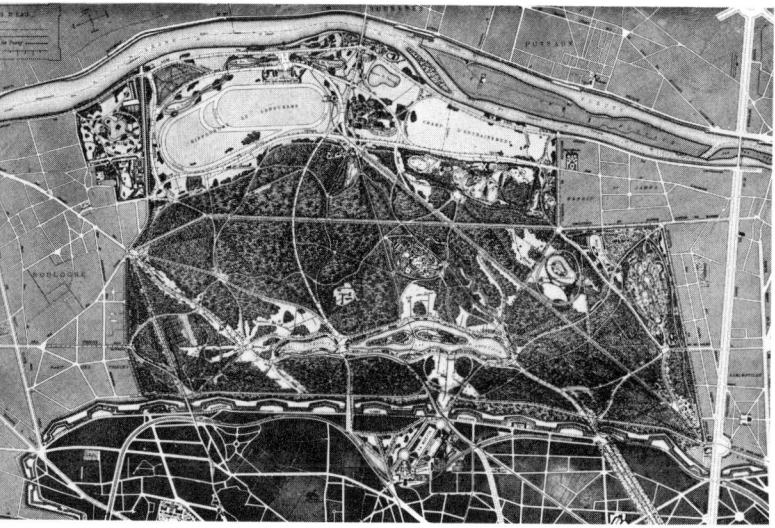

25. Avenue de l'Impératrice (now Avenue Foch), c. 1870, view and plan. This is the access boulevard to the Bois de Boulogne through the Porte Dauphine, bottom left.

26. Bois de Vincennes, c. 1870. View from the Plateau de Gravelle.

27. Sewers before Haussmann. (From Texier.)

28. Yonne aqueduct crossing the Yonne valley, January, 1873.

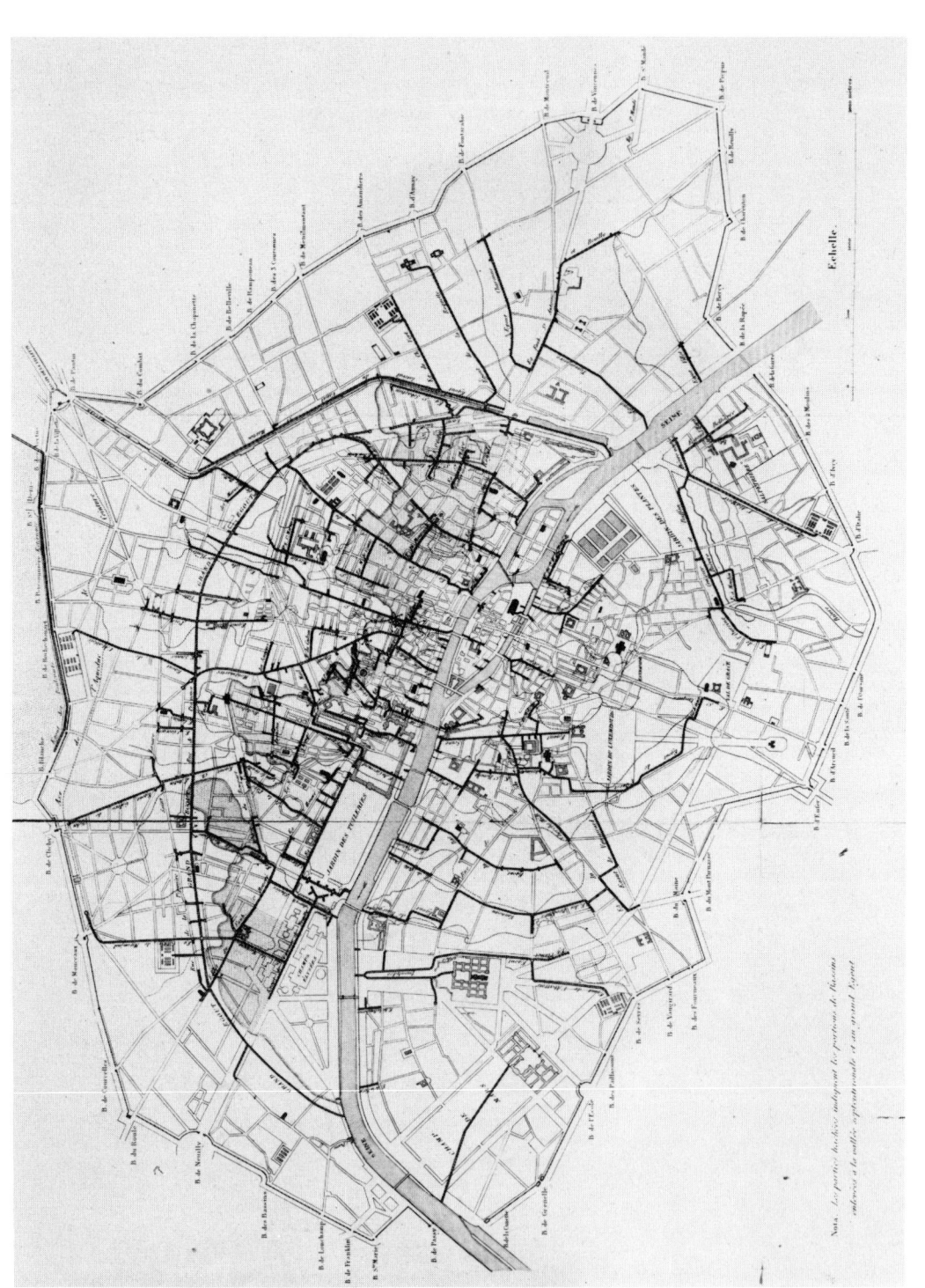

29. Sewer system before Haussmann, plan of January 1, 1837. Note that all sewers flow into the Seine within the city limits.

30. Collectors' sewers, plan of 1878. Note also the cemeteries: (1) Cimetière du Nord (now Cimetière Montmartre), (2) Cimetière Père-Lachaise, (3) Cimetière du Sud (now Cimetière Montparnasse). (4) Collectors' sewer at Asnières.

31. Roman baths of Constantius Chlorus, fourth century A.D. (Musée Cluny, Paris.)

32. Typical Parisian apartment house of the Second Empire, elevation and plans. (From *The Builder,* London, XVI [March 6, 1858], p. 159.)

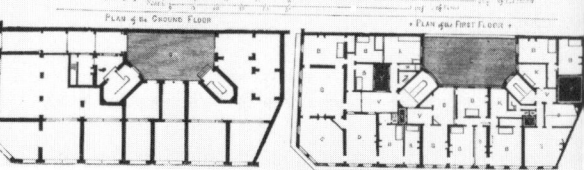

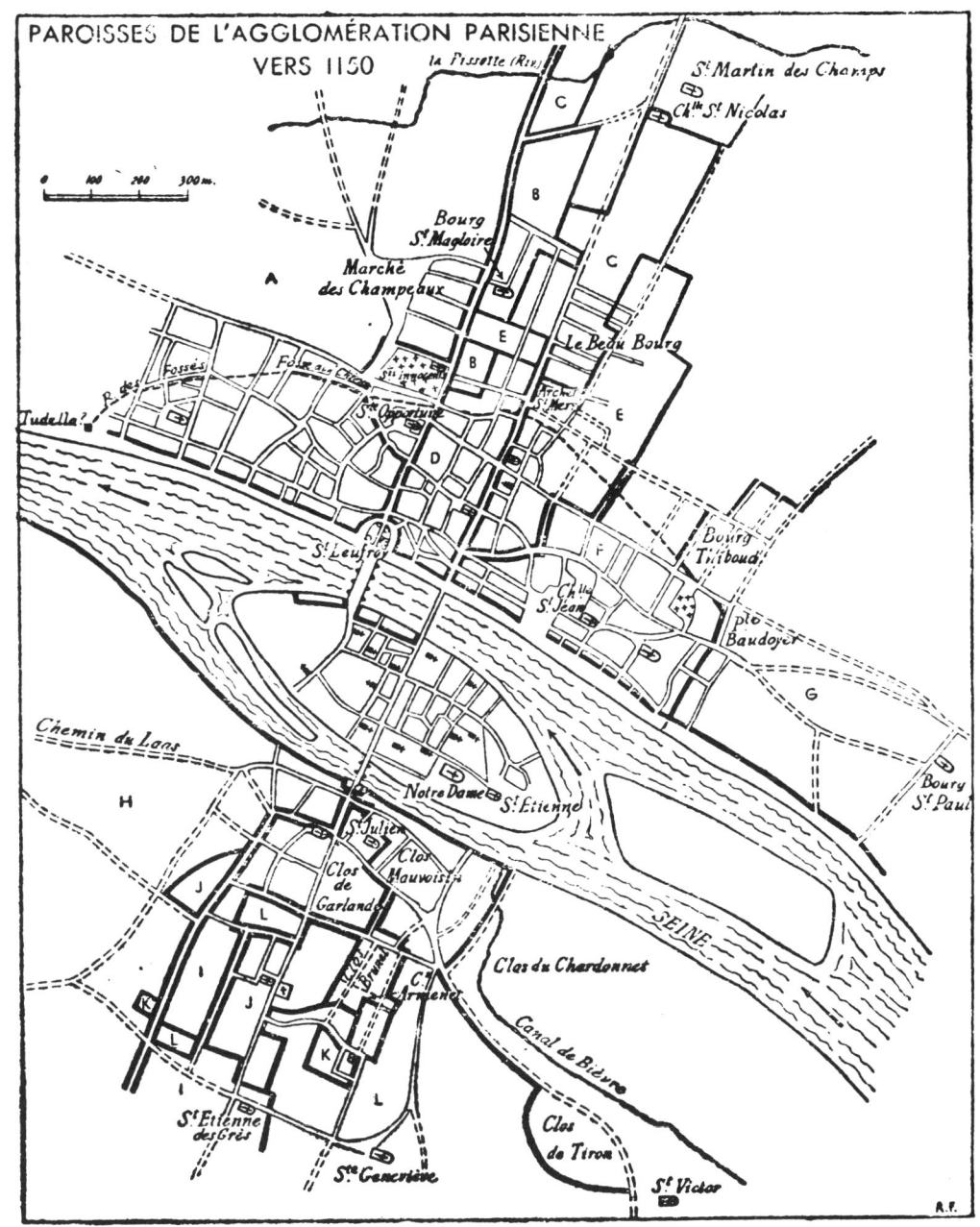

33. Paris, c. 1150, after Abbé Friedmann. The Marché des Champeaux (later Les Halles) is just north of the eleventh–twelfth-century town. Note parishes of Bourg Saint-Germain-des-Prés (H) and Bourg Sainte-Geneviève (L).

34. Parisian parishes of c. 1292, as shown in Junie plan of c. 1783. Ile de la Cité and bridges are reconstructed to pre-sixteenth-century state. Note: (1) Jardin du Roi, (2) la Grant Rue (later Rue St.-Denis), (3) Grand Pont (now Pont-au-Change), (4) old Roman bridge, (5) Rue St.-Martin, (6) Place de Grève, (7) Petit Pont, (8) St.-Gervais, (9) St.-Jacques, (10) St-Germain-l'Auxerrois, (11) St.-Germain-des-Prés, (12) Les Halles, (13) Cimetière des Saints-Innocents, (14) St.-Magloire, (15) St.-Merry, (16) St.-Martin-des-Champs, (17) Knights of the Temple (Templiers), (18) Louvre, (19) Porte Saint-Honoré, (20) wall of Philip Augustus, (21) "Ile de Notre Dame" (now Ile Saint-Louis).

35. Paris, Merian view, 1620. (1) Place Royale (later Place des Vosges) and (2) Place Dauphine are complete. (3) The Palais des Tuileries (after 1563–1564) is outside wall of Charles V at bottom center. (4) Hôpital St.-Louis is at top left.

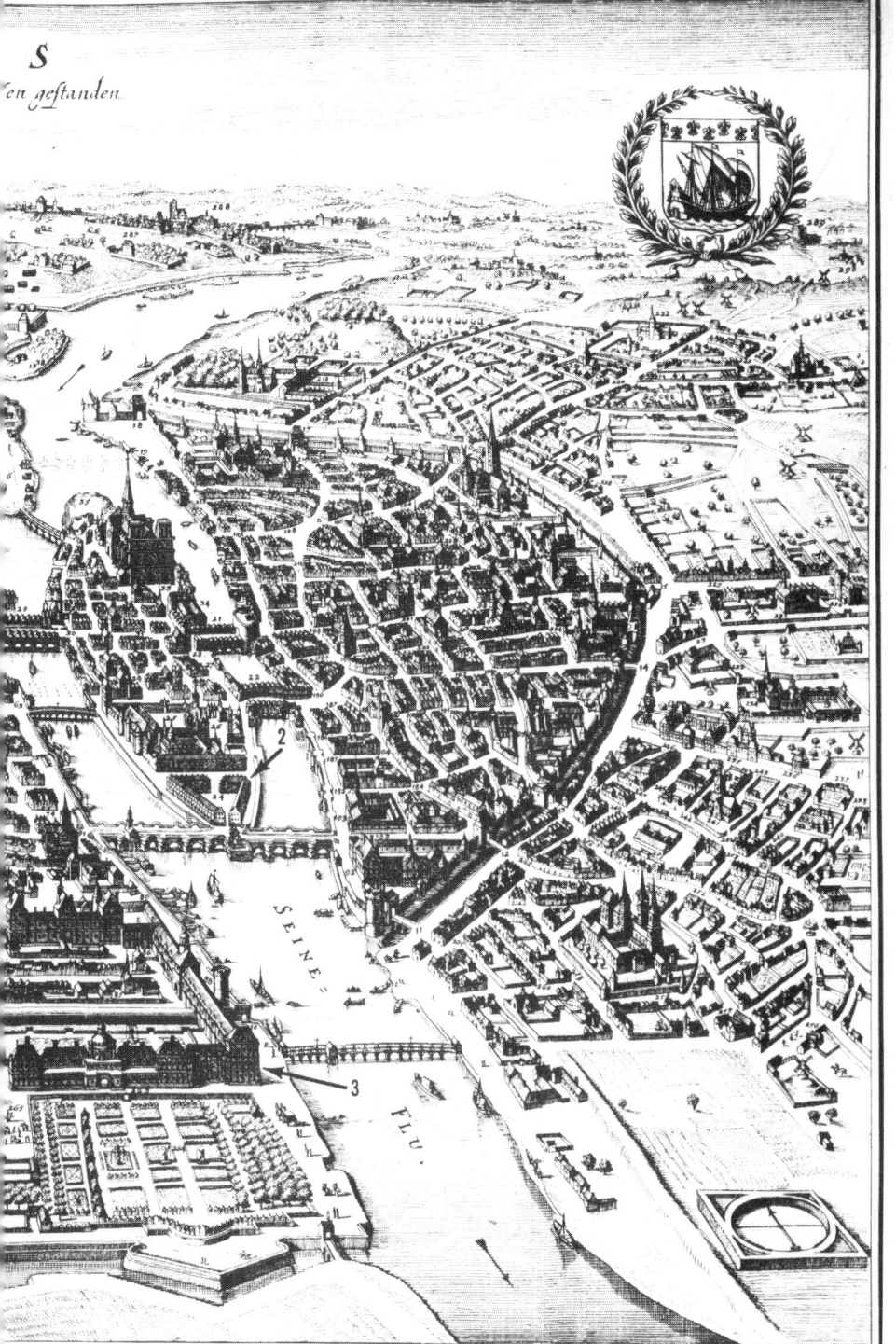

36. P. L. Debucourt: *Fête aux Halles*, 1782. (Musée Carnavalet, Paris.)

37. Paris, "Trois Personnages" view, 1538. (1) Note wall of Philip Augustus (c. 1200) is still preserved on Right Bank. (2) Ile de Louviers (a) and Ile de Notre Dame (b) east of Ile de la Cité, later combined to form Ile Saint-Louis, are still undeveloped. (3) Abbey of St.-Germain-des-Prés and the (4) Foire Saint-Germain are outside walls at lower right.

38. Limbourg brothers: month of June from the *Très Riches Heures*, c. 1415. In the background, western end of Ile de la Cité with former Palais-Royal and gardens. The Ste.-Chapelle is at right. (Musée Condé, Chantilly.)

39. Pierre Denis Martin: *Louis XV Crossing the Courtyard of Ste.-Chapelle* (September 12, 1715). (Musée Carnavalet, Paris.)

40. French, seventeenth-century: *Cimetière des Saints-Innocents.* In the right background is the tower of St.-Jacques-la-Boucherie. (Musée Carnavalet, Paris.)

41. Place de Grève and fourteenth-century Hôtel de Ville. (From *Missal de Jouvenal des Ursins*, 1450, Bibliothèque Historique de la Ville de Paris.)

42. Hôtel de Ville, sixteenth century. (Bibliothèque Nationale, Paris.)

43. East end of Paris, detail from Turgot plan, 1734. Bastille is left of center, near Porte Saint-Antoine, Place Royale (now Place des Vosges) below. Hôtel de Bretonvilliers is at upper tip of Ile Saint-Louis. Note Pont Marie and Pont de la Tournelle.

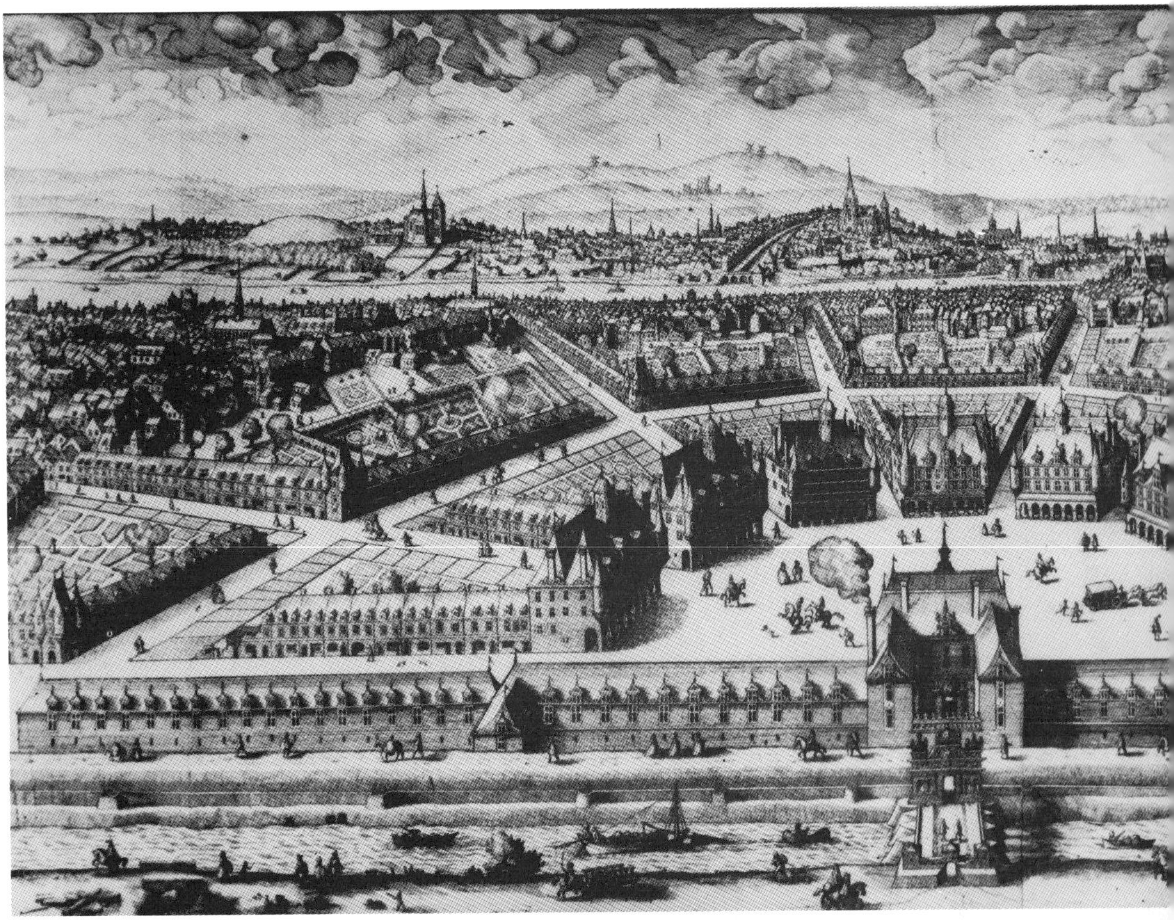

44. Place des Vosges (formerly Place Royale), showing house of Victor Hugo, present state.

45. Claude Chastillon and Jacques Alleaume: View of proposed Place de France, 1610. (From Chastillon, *Topographie Française.*)

46. Place Dauphine with Pont Neuf in foreground. Note transformation of original houses at right.

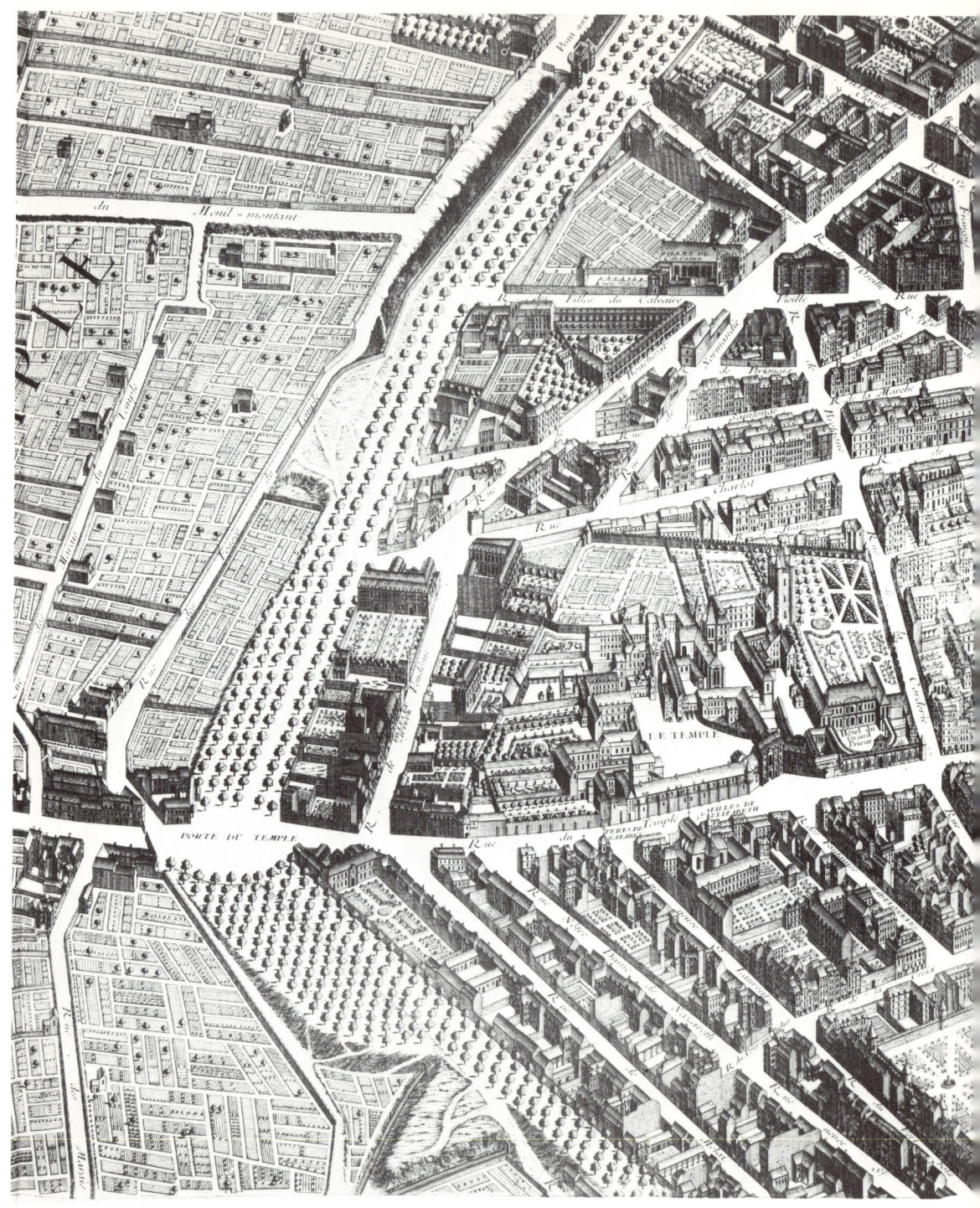

47. Quarter around the Porte du Temple. Walled compound of the Knights Templars at right center. The Place de France was planned to go directly behind the Temple. Rue Charlot and Rue de Boucherat (formerly Rue-Neuve Saint-Louis, now Rue de Turenne) are the only executed elements of the Place de France scheme. Porte du Temple is north. (Plan Turgot, 1734.)

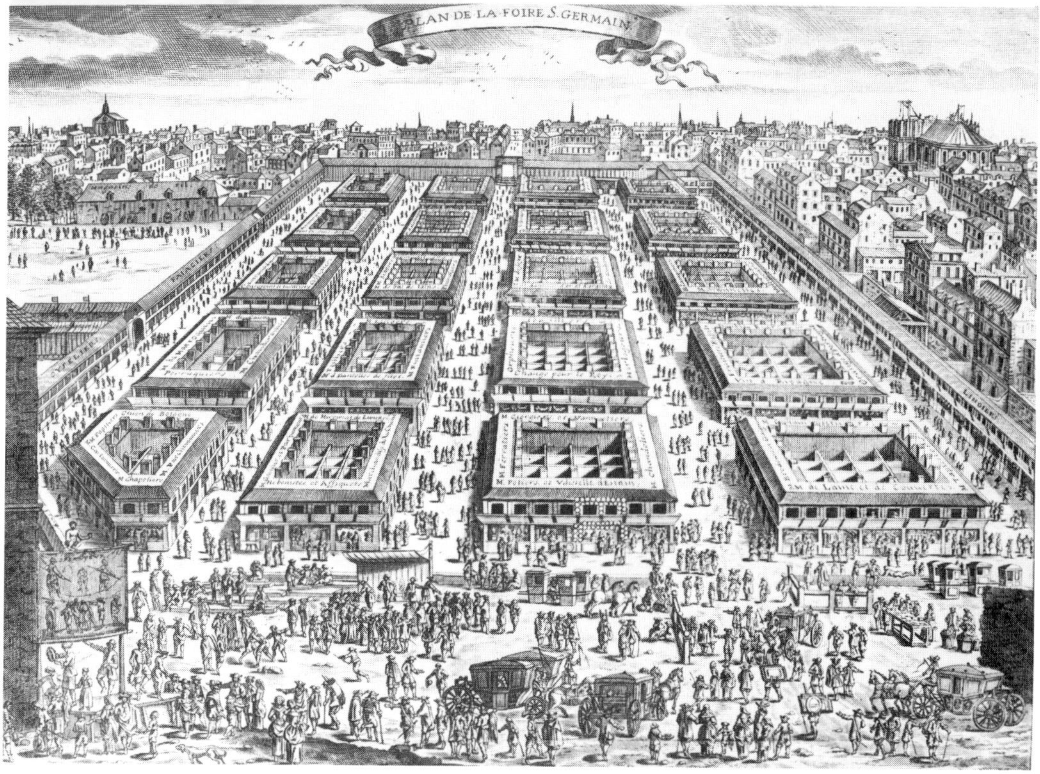

48. Saint-Germain markets, c. 1650. Church of St.-Sulpice (begun 1645) is in right background.

49. Ile Saint-Louis from the air. Diagonal bridge across eastern tip of island (Pont Sully) was constructed under Haussmann on an axis with the Panthéon (Ste.-Geneviève). Church of St.-Gervais and Hôtel de Ville (enlarged under Louis Phillipe) are in top center.

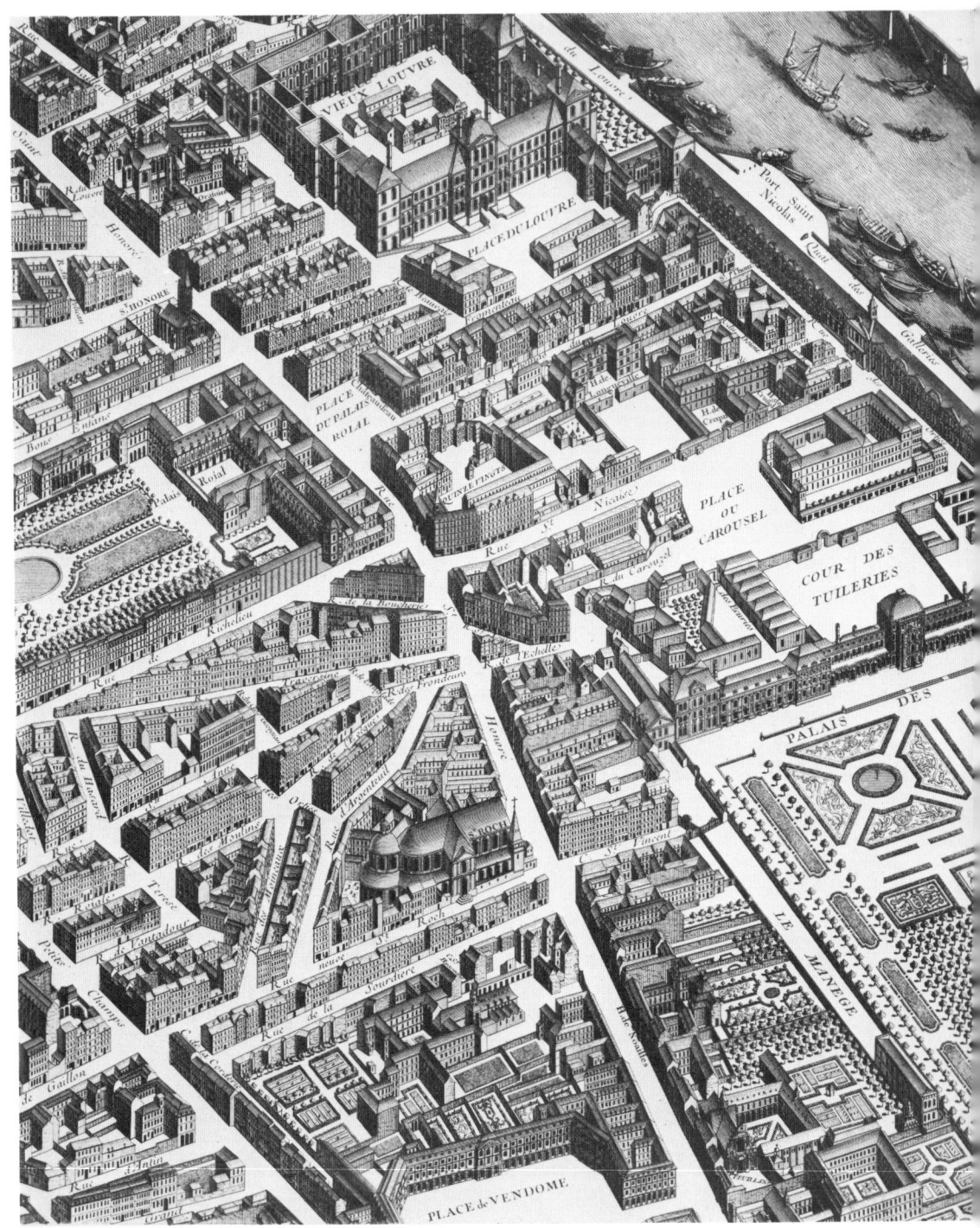

50. Louvre and the Faubourg Saint-Honoré. Hospice des Quinze-Vingts at center, corner Rue St.-Nicaise. Palais-Royal and Rue de Richelieu center left. Palais and Jardin des Tuileries lower right. (Plan Turgot, 1734.)

51. The Palais des Tuileries after its burning in 1871.

52. Palais du Luxembourg (begun 1615 by Salomon de Brosse) from the south, c. 1870. Its gardens had early become a public park.

53. Jean-Baptiste Oudrey: *Fire at Hôtel Dieu and Petit Pont, 1718*. Notre Dame Cathedral is in the background. (Musée Carnavalet, Paris.)

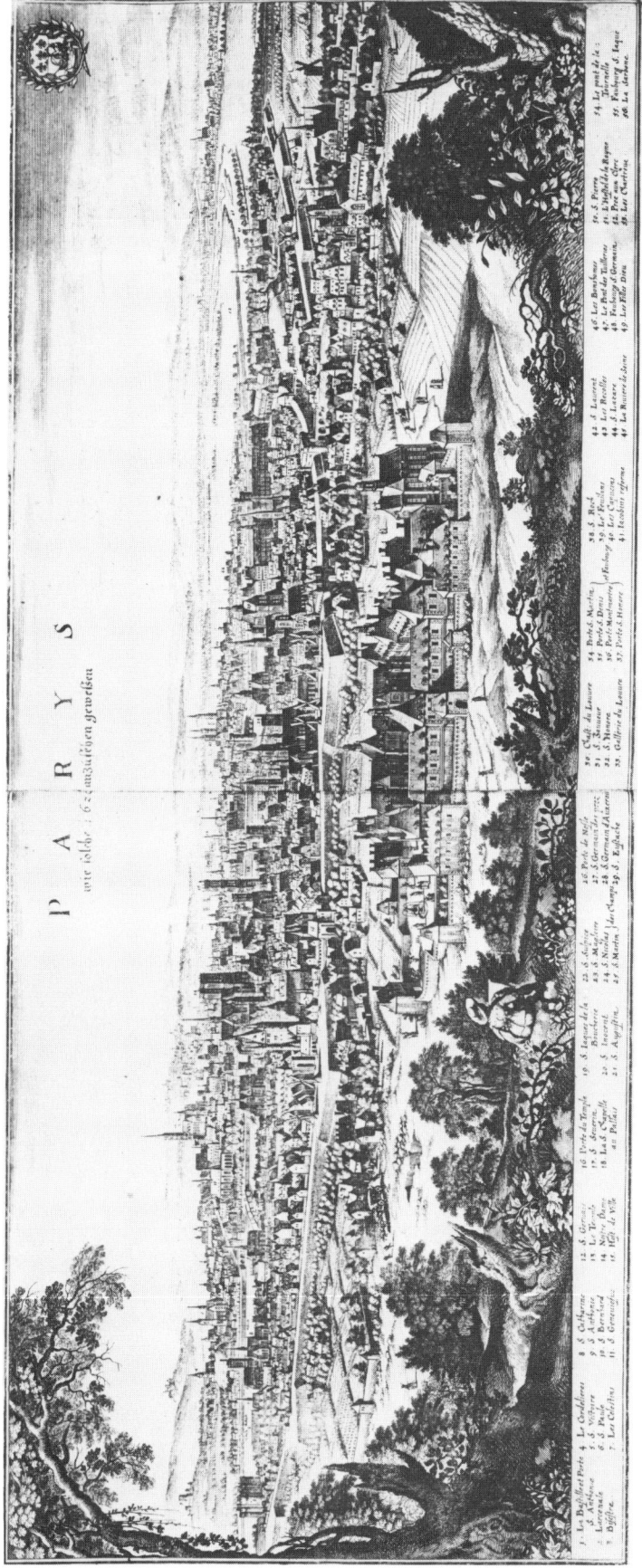

54. Paris, seen from north-east. Hôpital Saint-Louis (1607) in foreground. Note fortifications of Louis XIII extending at right around the Faubourg Saint-Honoré. (View by Merian, 1620.)

55. The Sorbonne. (From Texier.)

56. Jardin des Plantes. (From Texier.)

57. Hôpital de la Salpêtrière from the air. Chapel (lower right) by Libéral Bruant, c. 1670.

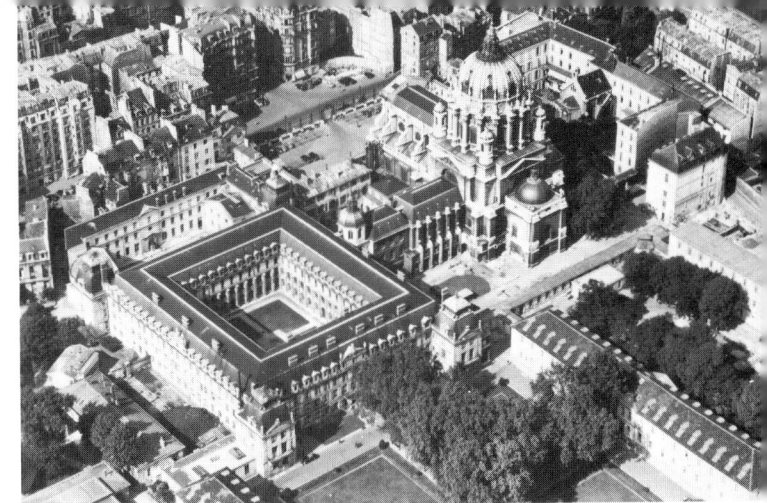

58. Church and convent of Val-de-Grâce (begun 1645), from the air.

59. Paris and environs, 1870, showing city wall of 1840. Dark lines mark main railroads into Paris. (1) Canal de l'Ourc, built under Napoleon I, (2) Saint-Denis, approximately ten miles north of Paris, (3) Versailles.

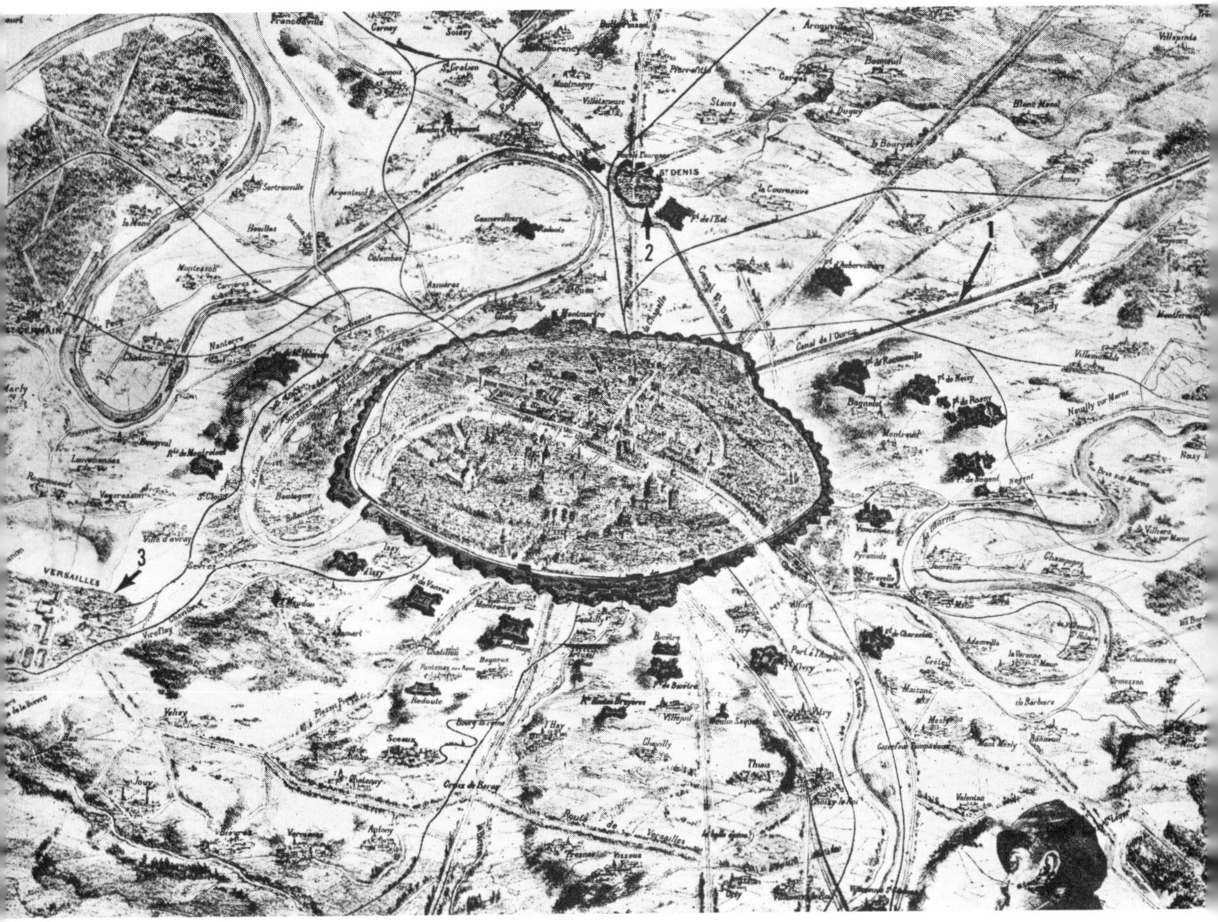

60. Balloon ascension of June 29, 1850, with Observatoire (begun in 1667 by Charles Perrault) in background. (From Texier.)

61. Observatoire from the air.

62. The Invalides (begun in 1670 by Libéral Bruant), from the west. Church by Jules Hardouin-Mansart (1679–1701).

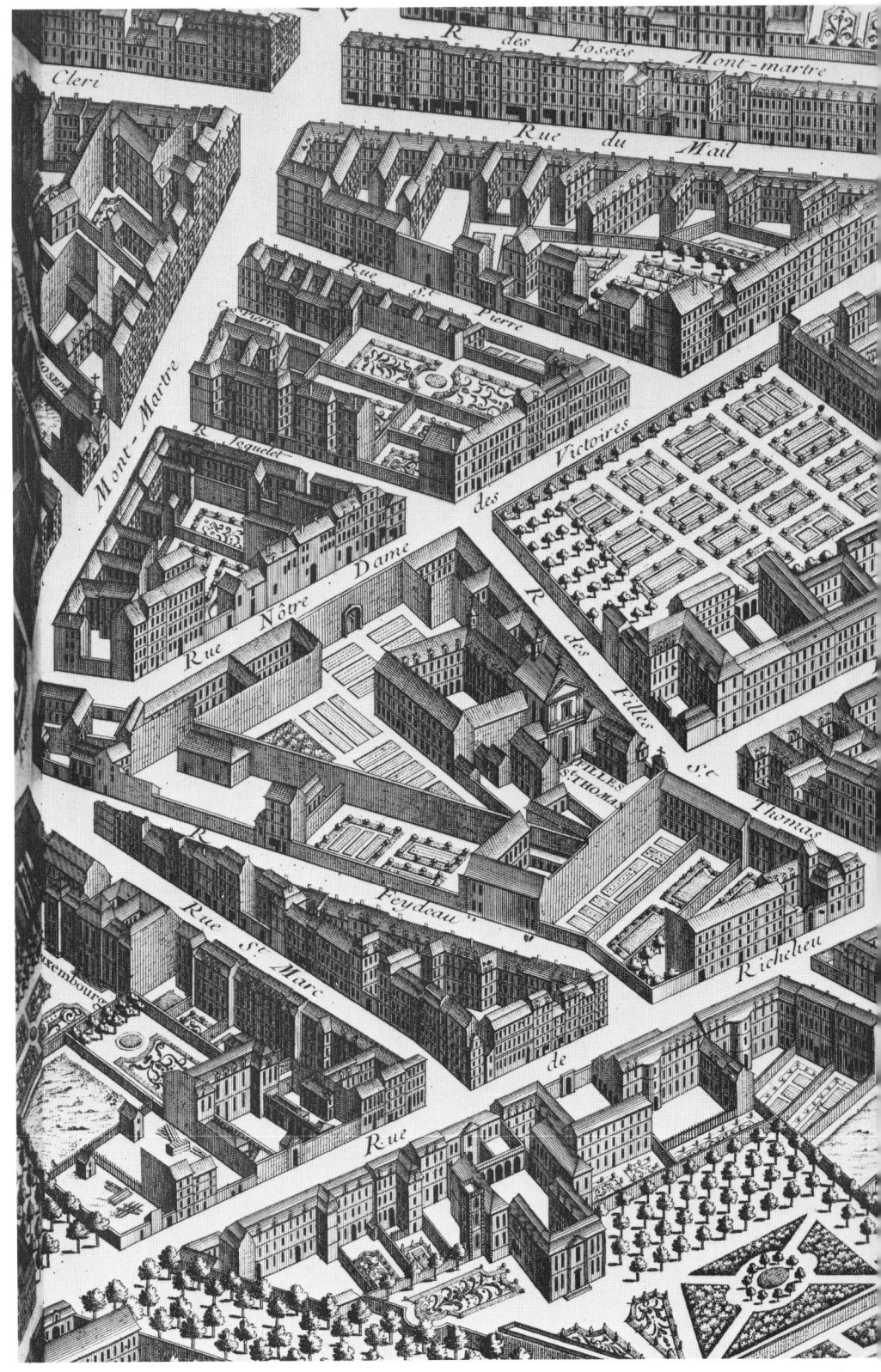

63. Place des Victoires, top center. Palais-Royal gardens, top right. Ex-Palais Mazarin, containing Bourse and Bibliothèque du Roi, at center on the Rue de Richelieu. (This view is left extension of *Fig. 50*.) (Plan Turgot, 1734.)

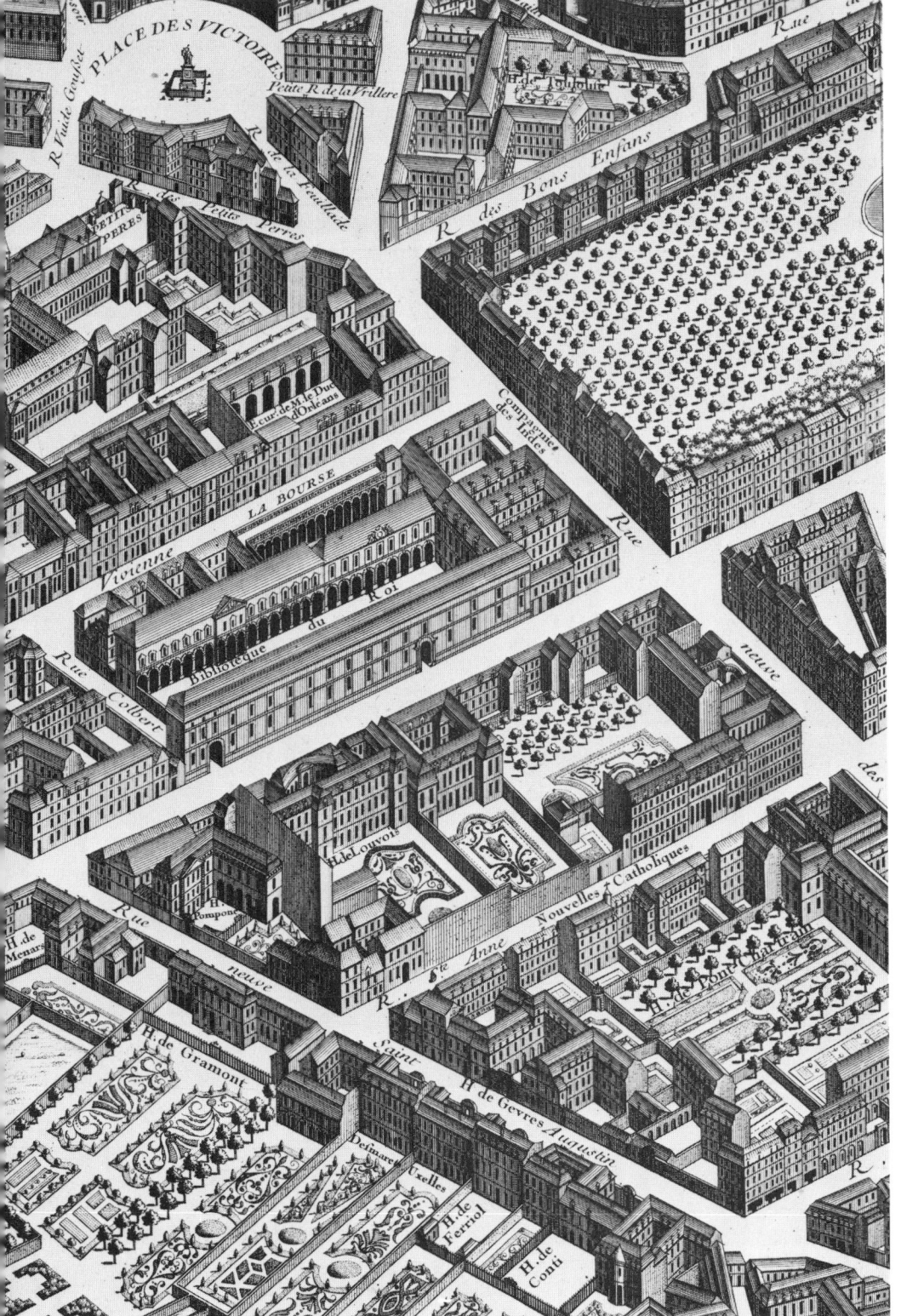

64. Place des Victoires (begun in 1685 by Mansart), detail from Turgot plan of 1734. East is at top. Rue des Fossés Mont-martre is now Rue d'Aboukir. Rue-Neuve des Petits-Champs is at lower right.

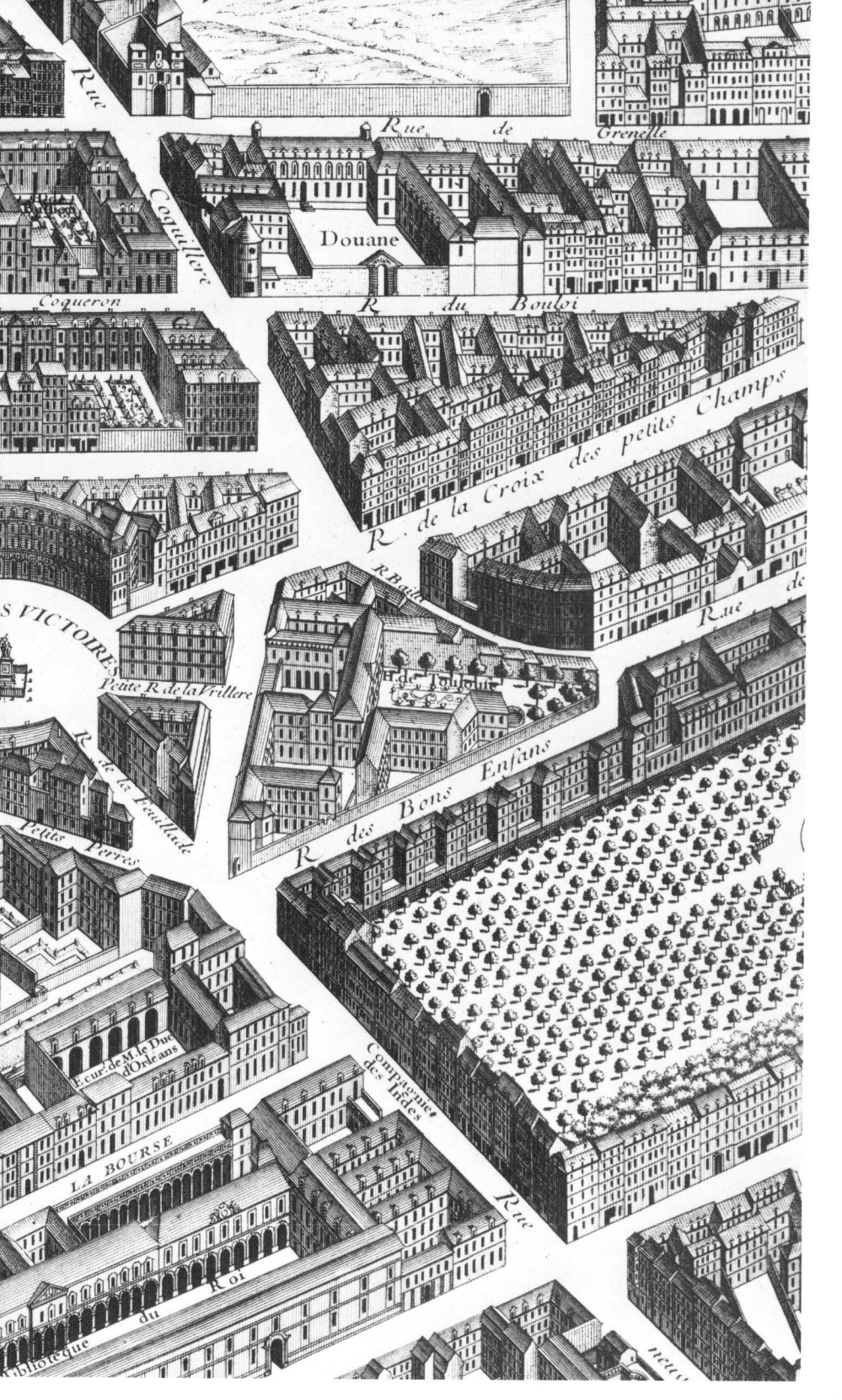

65. Place Vendôme. (From *Paris et les Parisiens au XIXe Siècle. Moeurs, Arts, et Monuments* [Paris, 1856.])

66. Palais and Jardin des Tuileries facing west. Champs-Elysées and the hill of Chaillot in background. Faubourg Sainte-Honoré at right. (Engraving by Mariette, late 17th century.)

67. Champ-de-Mars and École Militaire (1751), 1777. (Engraved by Lespinasse.)

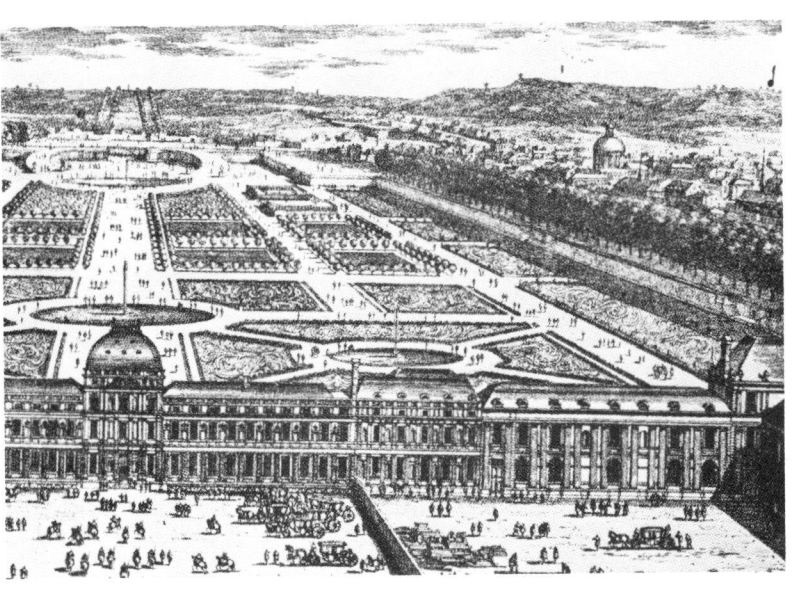

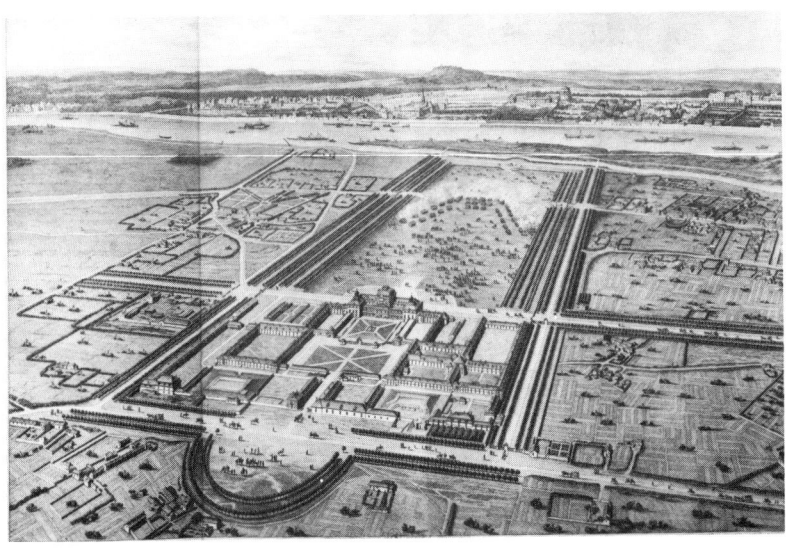

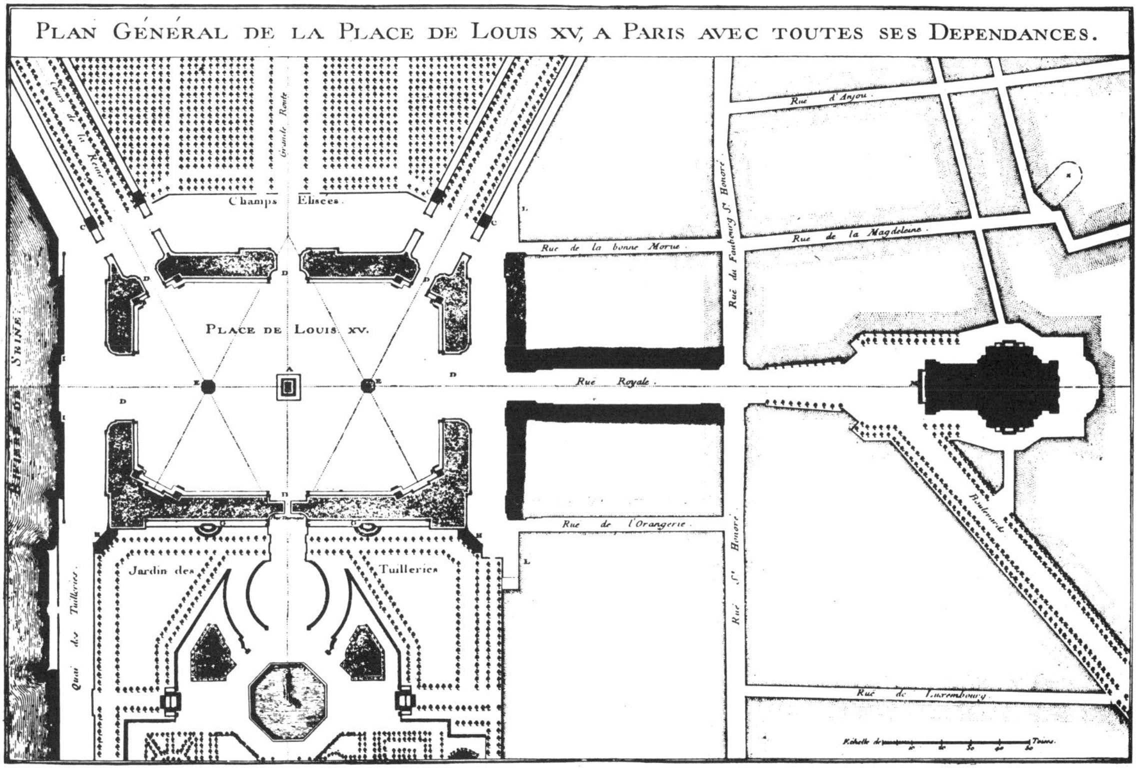

68. Jacques-Ange Gabriel: Place de la Concorde, begun in 1753. Above, view (Seine at bottom). Below, plan (Seine at left).

69. Place de la Concorde. Moats at the edges were filled in and the obelisk erected under J.-I. Hittorf. The church of the Madeleine on its Place is north of Rue St.-Honoré. (From Texier.)

70. Execution of Louis XVI in the Place de la Concorde, January 21, 1793. Engraved by Berthault. (Private collection.)

71. Place de la Concorde, from the air. The Jardins des Tuileries are in center, Rue de Rivoli at left, and Pont de la Concorde at lower right.

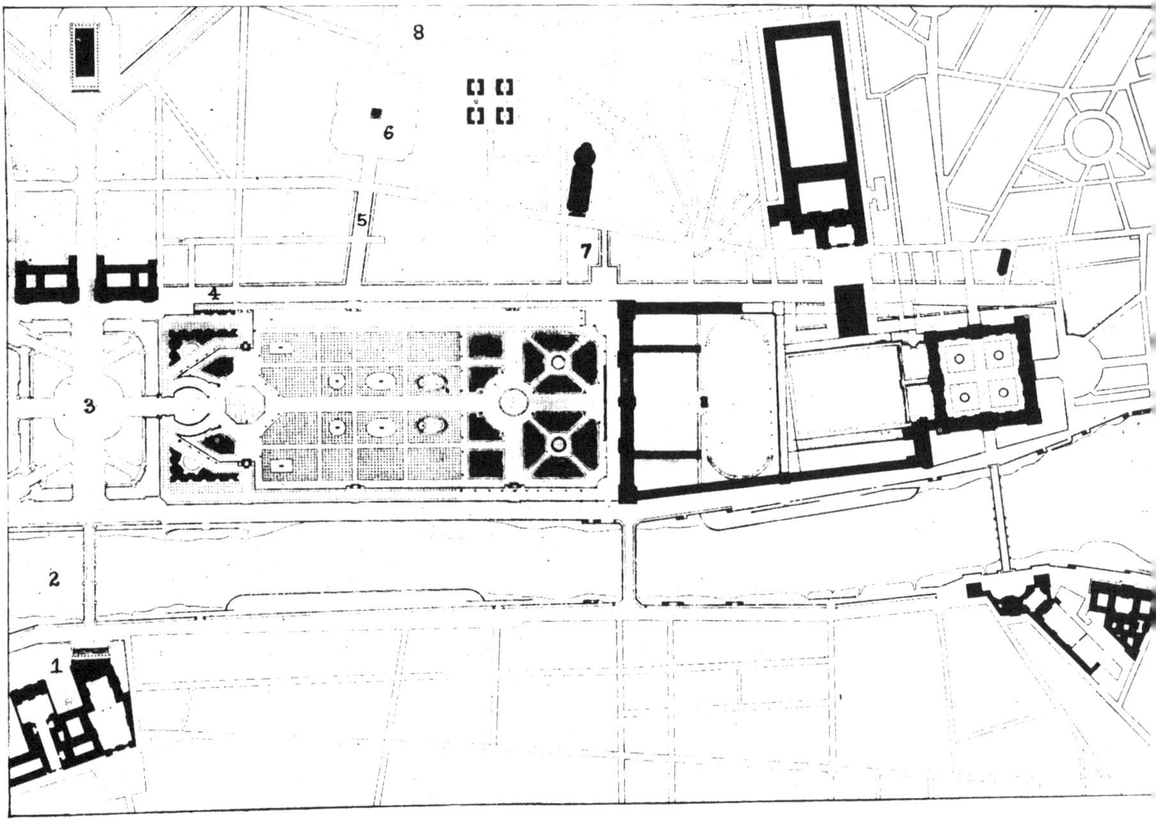

72. Plan of Napoleon I for the Rue de Rivoli. (1) Palais Bourbon, (2) Pont de la Concorde, (3) Place de la Concorde, (4) Rue de Rivoli, (5) Rue Castiglione, (6) Place Vendôme, (7) Rue des Pyramides, (8) Rue-Neuve des Petits-Champs. (From Percier and Fontaine, *Monuments de Paris*.)

73. Gosse: *Napoleon I Looking at Plans by his Architects, Percier and Fontaine.* (Collection Morel d'Arleux, Paris.)

74. Rue Royale with view of church of the Madeleine, c. 1900.
75. Claude-Nicolas Ledoux: Barrières (toll-gates) of the Champs-Elysées, 1791

76. Paris from the west, 1889. International Exposition with Eiffel Tower is at lower right. Arc de Triomphe and Avenue de Champs-Elysées are in center. Gare du Nord and Gare de l'Est are at top left. Panthéon (Ste.-Geneviève) and Val-de-Grâce are at top right.

77. Paris, c. 1850, surrounded by the wall of 1840.

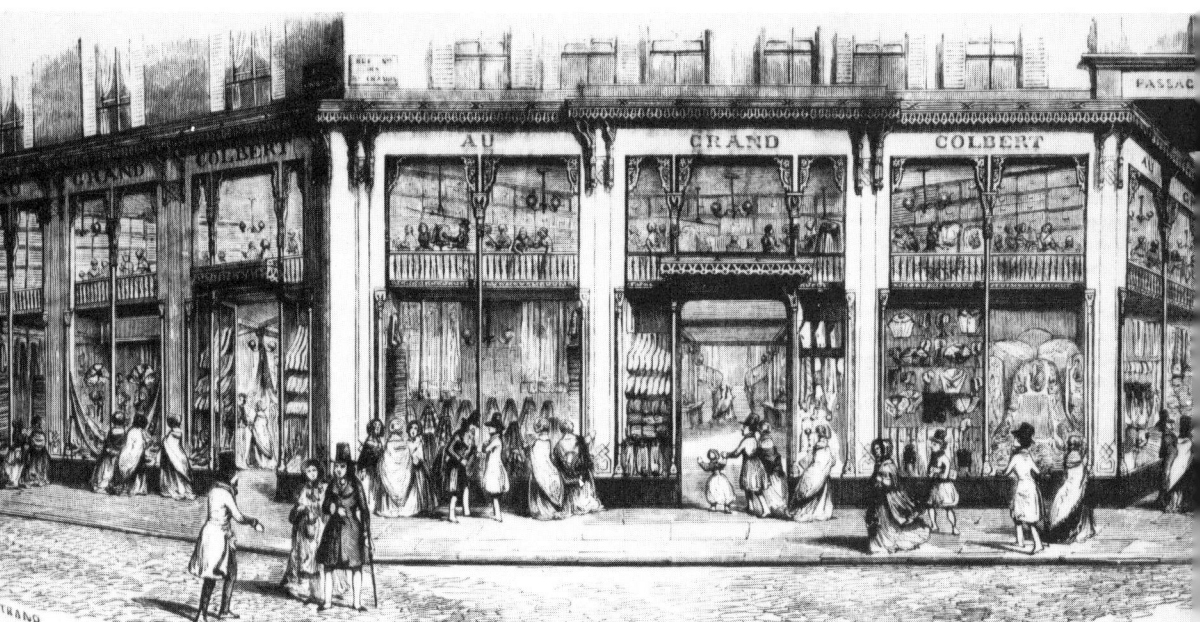

78. Boulevard Poissonière looking north up Rue du Faubourg-Montmartre. (From Texier.)

79. Magasins du Grand Colbert, on Rue-Neuve des Petits-Champs. (From Texier.)

80. The first Maison du Bon Marché, at the corner of Rue de Bac and Rue de Sèvres. (Collection Sirot, Paris.)

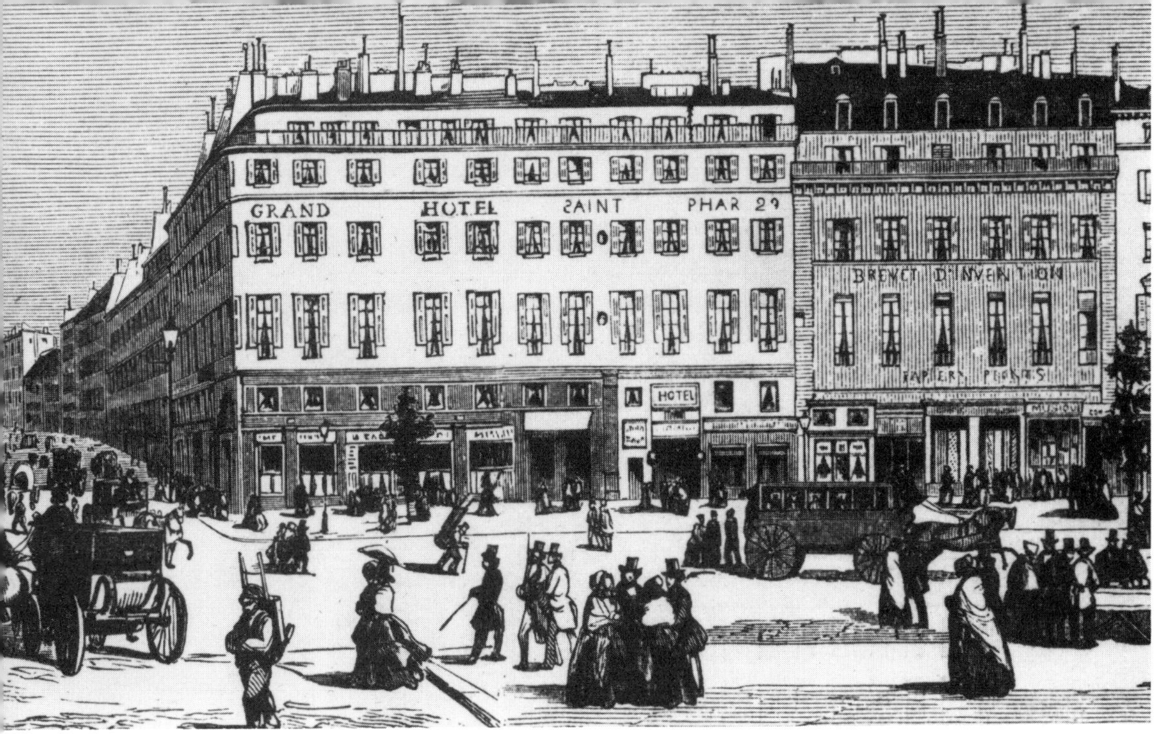
GRAND HOTEL SAINT PHAR
BREVET D'INVENTION
HOTEL

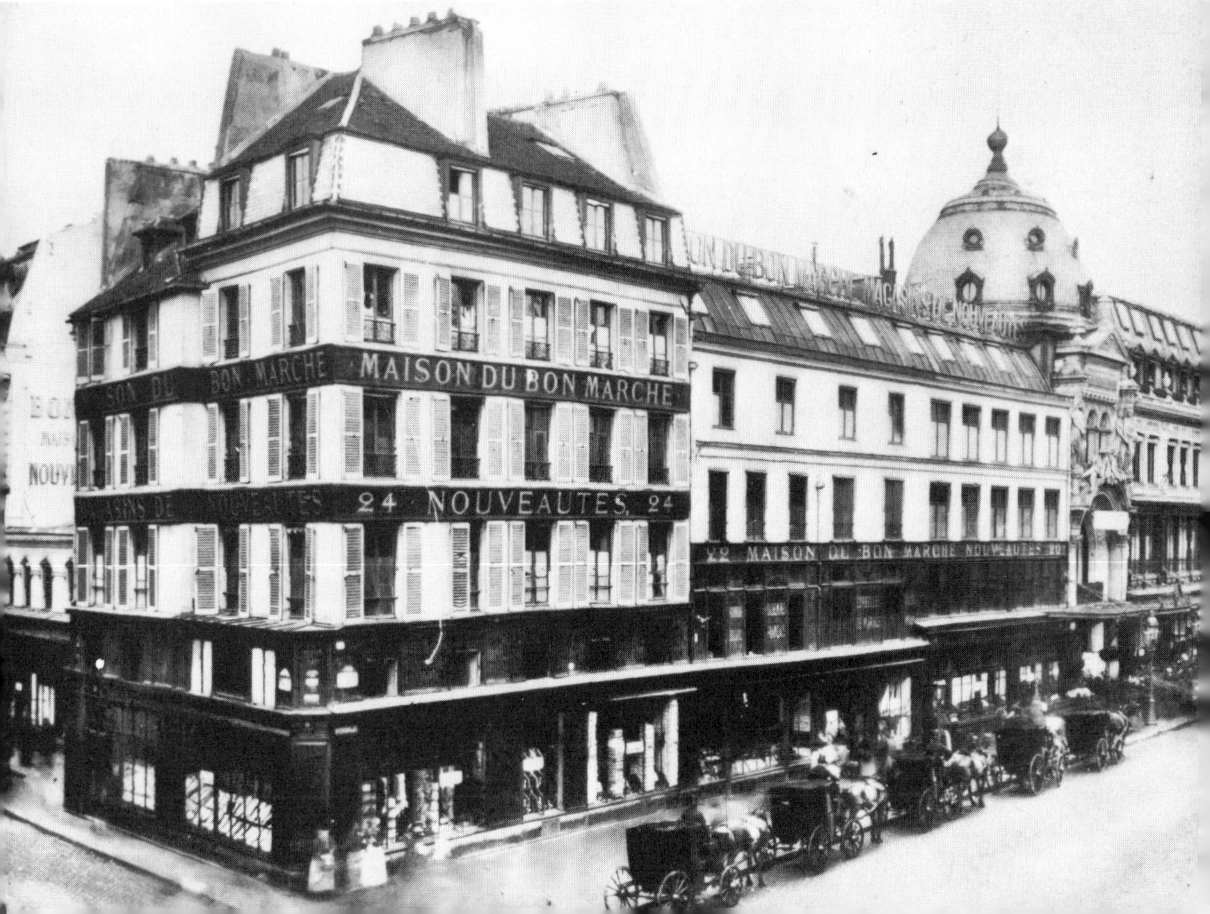
MAISON DU BON MARCHE
24 NOUVEAUTES 24
MAISON DU BON MARCHE NOUVEAUTES

81. Théâtre-Lyrique. (From Texier.)

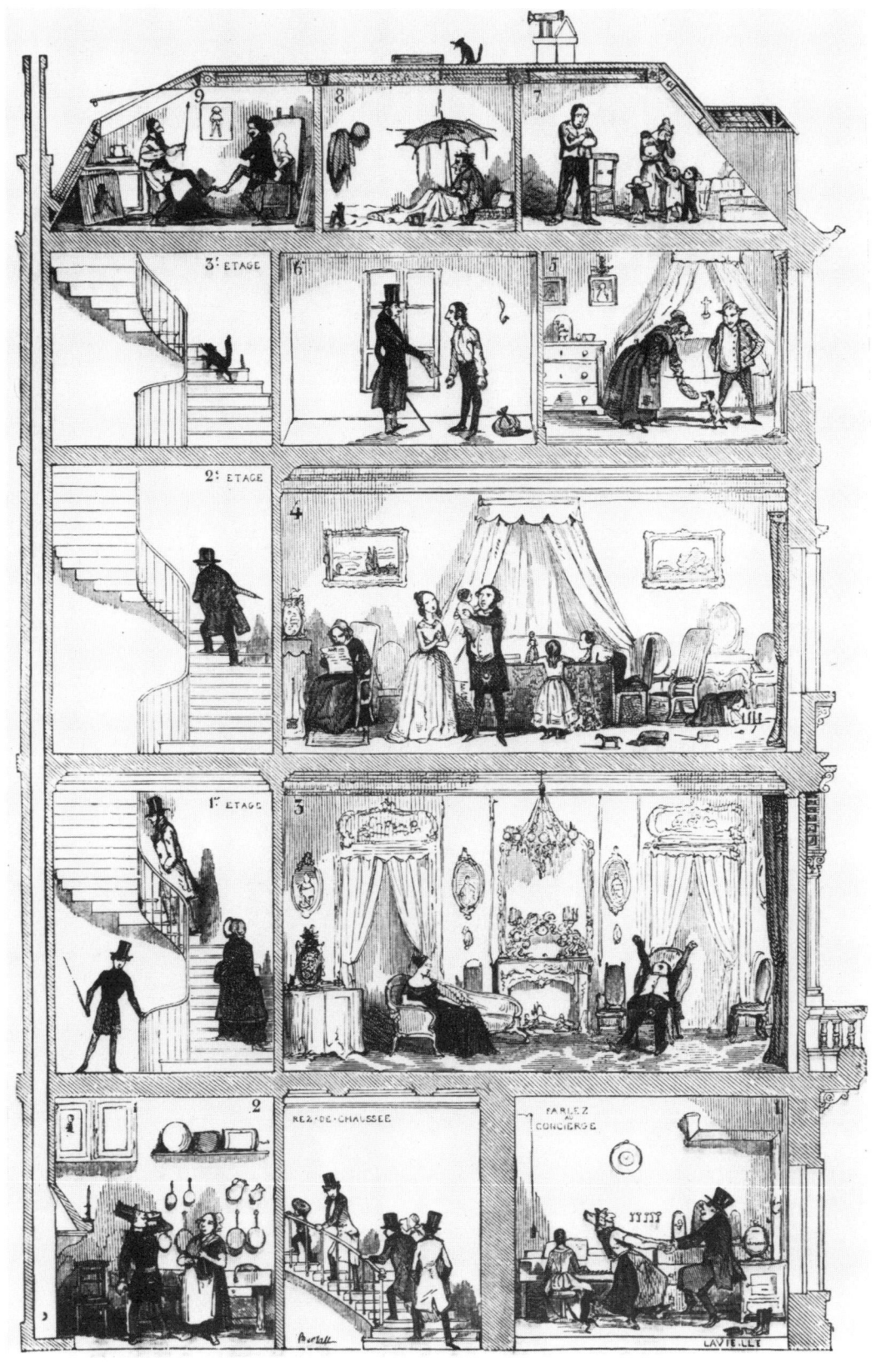

82. "Five Levels of Parisian Life."
(From Texier.)

83. Confectioner's shop. (From Texier.)

84. Charles Garnier: Opéra, completed 1875, longitudinal section. (From *Le Monde Illustré* [February 6, 1875].)

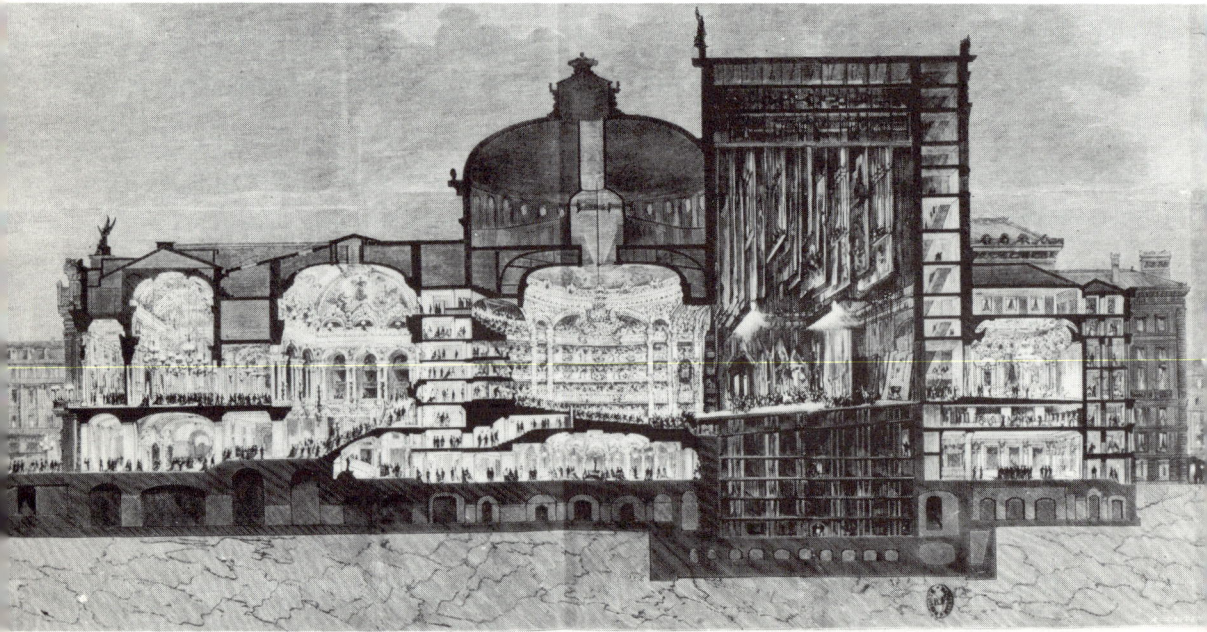

85. Restaurant Pied-de-Mouton, Rue Vauvilliers, c. 1890.

86. Café Moulin Rouge, at about the turn of the century.

87. Boulevard Richard-Lenoir, 1861–1863. (Reproduced from Gideon, *Space, Time, and Architecture*.)

agriculture were hostile to the deficit-financing policies of the regime as such. The Republicans were stifled by the limitations on suffrage and the controlled press. Disgruntled legitimists and ex-Orléanists were happy to fish in troubled waters. The Socialists saw no hope until the Empire was overthrown. Any and all of these groups seized every opportunity for criticism and gradually grew into an effective opposition. Haussmann, without a political base except the Emperor's uncertain personal support, was a prime symbolic target for attacks aimed at the regime itself. The fact remains that the urban bourgeoisie in general and the upper middle class in particular approved, participated in, and profited by the Haussmannization of Paris. The new class of daring financiers, large-scale building contractors, big department store owners, hotel operators, and the rest of the *nouveau riche* commercial breed had every reason to support and promote all aspects of the Second Empire program. These were men, after all, who lived, speculated, and grew with the growth of Paris, France, and Europe. Sound currency, adequate reserves, and other old-fashioned financial conventions gave them little concern. Deficit financing held no terrors for them because future profits promised to outstrip all present risks and deficits. Big business and the employed workers as well supported Napoleon III and Haussmann even if the lower middle class in the city and the provinces did not. It was in the national legislature with its heavily provincial representation that the opposition came and gradually gained the support of disaffected urban elements as Napoleon overextended his national goals and international ambitions. It was not, in the last analysis, a struggle between an eternally thickheaded bourgeoisie and the enlightened but isolated Prefect of the Seine, but the old and familiar battle between city and country.

Some of Napoleon's own ministers opposed the greenbelt scheme, an idea for which neither Napoleon nor Haussmann were prepared to fight and die. Haussmann hints at a possible conflict of interests in favor of unnamed clients.[34] This may not be unfounded, but the interests of these clients were in favor of building up this valuable land adjacent to the growing city. They won their point for the perfectly good reason that a city with an ever-growing population and a respectable group of urban parks in the process of development simply could not afford to constrict its rapidly expanding suburbs with a wide expanse of open space. As a matter of fact, Paris already had quite enough large breaks in its urban fabric. The suburbs would surely have grown, in fact they have grown, well beyond that proposed ring of greenery, and the avenues beyond a greenbelt would have been even more hopelessly isolated from the center of town than they are now.[35]

Finally, two crucial and essentially interrelated aspects of the attack on Second Empire housing must be considered: the condemnation of the intermingling of functions in the Parisian apartment house and the "wardrobe" critique of the boulevards behind which "the most appalling disorder lies concealed" (*Fig. 87*). I would suggest that in these two aspects lies the secret of Haussmann's success.

It apparently never occurred to either Napoleon or Haussmann, in their most extravagant dreams of demolition, to pull down all of old Paris in order to rebuild it anew. They wanted to improve the city, not destroy it. What lies behind the new boulevards was neither "appalling disorder" nor unspeakable slums, but the tightly knit, highly organic, and lively fabric of the old town which was just as essential to the everyday life of all Parisians as were the new boulevards. After all, the upper middle class bourgeois did not live by champagne and lobster alone, but by bread, sausages, and red wine as well and plain cotton goods, old books, and the products of artisan labor and small shopkeepers, too. But these items were not to be had in the expensive new stores and cafés along the boulevards. Rents and overhead were much too high for the survival of such commerce there. These things were to be found just around the corner in the narrow streets and old houses left standing behind the great streets with their fine new buildings. And most of the people who ran that part of the urban economy lived there too, right on top of or near the shops. By design or by sheer commonsense laissez-faire, urban dislocation was kept to a minimum in Haussmann's colossal city renewal.

If the wardrobe theory were correct and Haussmann—willy-nilly—left his great work of demolition half undone, then the most successful quarters of Paris ought to be the new *arrondissements* of the periphery where little or nothing stood in the way of a total development along Haussmann's lines; for example, the new quarters laid out toward Neuilly and Les Batignolles around the Parc de Monceau with their major arteries, the Boulevards Malesherbes and Pereire and the Avenue Wagram running north from the Place de l'Étoile. The fact is that, on the contrary, the inner quarters of the city—with their integrated mixture of large regular new streets and narrow irregular old streets, with their complex intermingling of variously scaled commercial and residential functions—are still the most successful and agreeable parts of the city from every point of view. The city that Haussmann found in 1850 being already large, Paris preserves to this day one of the largest successful urban areas of any city in the world. Urban failure in Paris begins in varying degrees at precisely those points where the network of Haussmann's streets runs beyond the periphery of the old city.

The old phenomenon of the Place des Vosges repeated itself again (pp. 34–35). The new quarters survived and were successful in exactly the measure to which they were close to and in intimate contact with the active and living urban core. Their existence was for a considerable period a semi-parasitic one, just as that of the old Place des Vosges had been. If the Parc de Monceau and Place de Ternes quarters had and continue to have a certain fashionable quality and success, it is in good part because they are closer to the active center than other similar quarters and because they are interlaced with older surviving suburban streets such as the Rue du Faubourg Saint-Honoré and the Rue de Courcelles which, with their shops and houses, wound their way out of the old city toward the tax farmers' wall well before the Pereire brothers and their like stimulated Haussmann's development of this area.

The other new peripheral *arrondissements* in the south, north, and east, where Haussmann's and his successors' new streets crisscross each other without the presumed liability of ancient "slums" hidden away behind them, are even drearier. Tourists seldom see them and, in fact, there is not much to see except the present-day Parisian *Lumpenproletariat* of Moroccans, Algerians, and black Africans. These desperate people are there not because the city has succeeded but because it has failed. There is no use blaming bad housing and unscrupulous landlords. The question is, why did these quarters succumb to squalor and dullness so easily? If anything saves these parts of Paris from the utter horror of similar residential quarters in London and so many European and American cities, it is precisely the old French tradition, derived from the ancient Roman apartment house and continued in Haussmann's buildings, of mingling commercial and residential functions as well as various economic and social levels under one roof (*Fig. 82*).

PARIS SINCE HAUSSMANN

Some 60 percent of the buildings and streets of present-day Paris were built in Haussmann's time. But the Paris of 1970 is not the Paris of 1870. The very success of the nineteenth-century developments created new problems. That the commercial base—the productive goose behind the golden egg of every city—has grown, infiltrated, and gradually saturated the core of Haussmann's Paris to its limits at the Étoile and beyond in the west and up to and beyond the Place de la Nation in the east is hardly a sign of urban failure.

But the integration achieved a century ago has not been and probably could not be maintained. The progressive segregation of the wealthier classes in the west and the working classes in the north and east, accelerated by the commercial expansion at the core, has exacerbated social tension in Paris and created new problems of public transportation and administration. Haussmann did nothing either to speed up or to deter this trend which had its origins in Francis I's move to the west and the gradual growth of the wealthier business and residential quarters around the Louvre and the Palais-Royal. Parks, large and small, monuments, churches, public buildings, sewers, water mains, and boulevards were distributed more or less equally throughout all parts of the city. Political pressure from the upper as well as the working classes saw to that. But the unpromising policy of using urban reconstruction as an instrument of social revolution was decidedly not part of Haussmann's or Napoleon III's thinking. For them the rebuilding of Paris was a matter of adjusting the city to the needs of their time, not to the uncertain ideals of a distant future. Later administrations have not departed spectacularly from this approach.

Better bus lines and perhaps the most logical and coherent subway system in the world have turned both the inner core and the less successful outskirts into viable entities. Haussmann would have liked that subway! The outlying suburban areas, increasingly popular as places of middle and lower middle class residence since the turn of the century, have been connected with the center by an efficient and inexpensive system of suburban railways.

The twentieth century has not left Haussmann's Paris unscathed. As elsewhere, the automobile is beginning to saturate even the generously proportioned streets built in the horse-and-carriage days of the Second Empire. Paris during the weekend rush hours is practically immobilized by traffic.

The evolution of Paris since 1870 and the various post-Haussmann projects for its further transformation, mostly and probably mercifully left unrealized by the pragmatic Parisians, deserve more than a brief summary statement. It is a field for further intensive study and evaluation.

Eugène Hénard (1849–1923) preceded Le Corbusier in proposing immense traffic throughways cutting across the heart of Paris. An enormously enlarged Rue de Richelieu would have been intersected by an east-west roadway sliced through the Palais-Royal gardens.[36] Le Corbusier never stopped making plans for Paris. A detailed consideration of his projects is beyond the scope of this study, but is treated in another volume in this series.[37] Let it be said only that Le Corbusier consistently concerned himself not with the periphery which was and is in trouble[38] but with the inner core of the city, that *îlot insalubre* which, he felt, needed uprooting and transformation, like the society which it served.

The history of Paris and Haussmann's experience would seem to offer one overriding lesson for present-day urban theorists and planners: A city is a living and growing organism, but not without its delicate side. It frequently needs more room in which to exercise its economic muscles. It is subject to fatigue, shortness of breath, hardening and blockage of the arteries, and occasionally to apoplexy. Aspirins and tranquilizers usually do not alleviate its ailments. It may require careful surgery of the heart, veins, and arteries and a steady diet of capital investment. Piecemeal transformations, carefully studied for their long-range effect on and interaction with surrounding areas, may leave ambitious planners, hungering for vast projects, unsatisfied, but they are more easily digested by the city and, if erroneous in conception, less disastrous to the sensitive urban fabric.

One thing is sure to kill the city: disembowelment.

NOTES

INTRODUCTION

1. See H. van Werveke, "The Rise of the Towns. Town Population," *The Cambridge Economic History of Europe*, Vol. III (Cambridge: University Press, 1963), p. 37f. See also A. F. Weber, *The Growth of Cities in the Nineteenth Century* (New York: Columbia University Press, 1899; and Ithaca: Cornell Reprints in Urban Studies, 1963).

2. For Pinkney, see Bibliography, p. 122.

3. For Alphand and Belgrand, see Bibliography, p. 122.

THE REBUILDING OF PARIS

4. For these projects, see John Summerson, *Georgian London* (New York, 1946; revised ed., 1962), pp. 177f.

5. L. Réau and Pierre Lavedan, *L'Oeuvre du Baron Haussmann, Préfet de la Seine* (1853–1870) (Paris, 1954), pp. 70f.

6. For a more detailed discussion, see David H. Pinkney, *Napoleon III and the Rebuilding of Paris* (Princeton: University Press, 1956), Chap. VI: "Paris Underground," pp. 127f.

7. Jules Ferry (1832–1893), lawyer, journalist, and statesman, opposed the régime of Napoleon III. Elected republican deputy in 1869, he was mayor of Paris during the long siege of 1870. He later held various important ministries, was premier in 1880–1881, fought for freedom of the press, secondary schooling for women, and was a proponent of French colonial expansion. A middle-of-the-road republican, he drew fire from both the political extreme right and left. At the time of his death he was president of the Senate.

CRITICAL EVALUATION: 1

8. For a brief discussion, see Lavedan's article, "L'influence de Haussmann: L'Haussmannisation" in *L'Oeuvre du Baron Haussmann*, pp. 142f. On Vienna: George R. and C. C. Collins, "The Transformation of Vienna," chap. 4 of *Camillo Sitte and the Birth of Modern City Planning* New York: Random House, 1965), pp. 34f. The character and effect of Haussmannesque urban transformations in major cities outside France remains to be studied in detail. See Françoise Choay, *The Modern City: Planning in the 19th Century* (Planning and Cities series) New York: George Braziller, Inc., 1969), pp. 15–22.

9. See Henry-Russell Hitchcock, *Architecture: Nineteenth and Twentieth Centuries* (Baltimore: Penguin Books, 1958; 2nd edition, 1963), pp. 131f.

10. For example, G. Pillement, *Destruction de Paris* (Paris, c. 1941).

11. Jane Jacobs, *The Death and Life of Great American Cities* (New York: Random House, 1961).

12. *The Culture of Cities* (New York: Harcourt, Brace, and Company, 1938).

13. See Sigfried Giedion, *Space, Time and Architecture* (Cambridge, Mass.: Harvard University Press, 1941 and later editions), particularly his chapters on Haussmann, which have created a renewal of interest in the subject.

14. *Ibid.*, 4th ed., 1962, pp. 668, 678.

15. *Ibid.*, p. 678.

16. *Ibid.*, pp. 671–672.

17. *Ibid.*, pp. 673–675.

18. *Ibid.*, p. 648.

19. *Ibid.*, p. 670.

20. It may be noted in passing that where socialist régimes have come to power in eastern Europe, they have generally been content to take over their large cities in the late-nineteenth–early-twentieth-century state in which they found them without major transformations of the functioning centers. Mussolini's urban projects in Rome and other Italian cities provided pomp, but little effective improvement.

MEDIEVAL PARIS

21. Paris celebrated its 2,500th anniversary in 1951. Its origins as a place of settlement go back well before the period under consideration here; but there are no visible remains from these earlier periods, and our purposes are served by beginning with the late antique town.

22. I cannot follow that astute student of medieval Paris and its parishes, the Abbé Friedmann (*Paris. Ses rues, ses paroisses du môyen age à la révolution*, Paris, 1959) in his suggestion that the Bourg Saint-Germain-l'Auxerrois was also enclosed in that first *enceinte*.

23. Adam Smith, "Rise of the Towns," in *An Inquiry into the Nature and Causes of the Wealth of Nations*, 1776.

24. For the role of the mendicant orders in the thirteenth and fourteenth centuries and the location of their churches, see the author's *Medieval Cities* (Planning and Cities series) (New York: George Braziller, Inc., 1968), pp. 40, 119, n. 16.

PARIS FROM 1500 TO NAPOLEON III

25. Concerning Brunelleschi's project for a Piazza di S. Spirito facing the Arno River, see Saalman, ed., *Antonio Manetti, The Life of Brunelleschi* (University Park, Pa., and London: Pennsylvania State University Press, 1970), p. 125, line 1511f. On Alberti, L. H. Heydenreich, "Pius II als Bauherr von Pienza," *Zeitschrift für Kunstgeschichte*, Vol. VI (1937), pp. 105–146; see also the author's "The Baltimore and Urbino Panels: Cosimo Roselli," *Burlington Magazine*, Vol CX (1968), p. 379. On Leonardo, see C. Pedretti, *A Chronology of Leonardo da Vinci's Architectural Studies after 1500* (Geneva, 1962), p. 112f (plan for Piazza S. Lorenzo-Via Larga in Florence). See also Leonardo Benevolo, *Storia dell' Architettura di Rinascimento*, 2 vols. (Bari, 1968), and Giulio C. Argan, *The Renaissance City* (Planning and Cities series) (New York: George Braziller, Inc., 1969).

26. Concerning the Place de France, see Gustave Pagniez in *Bulletin de la Société de l'Histoire de Paris et de l'Ile-de-France*, Vol. XXIV (1897), pp. 112–114. See also A. Poirson, *Histoire du Règne de Henri IV*, Vol. IV (Paris, 1846), pp. 518f, and L. Hautecoeur, "Place de France," in *Histoire de l'Architecture Classique en France*, Vol. I (1966, rev. ed.), pp. 302–305.

27. See Leon Battista Alberti, *De Re Aedificatoria,* ed. Orlandi (Milan, 1966), Vol. II, Book IX, Chap. 1; Andrea Palladio, *I Quattro Libri dell'Architettura* (Venice, 1570), Book II, Chap. 1; *Tutte l'Opere d'Architettura et Prospetiva di Sebastiano Serlio . . . raccolto da M. Gio. Domenico Scamozzi Vicentino* (Venice, 1619), pp. 126–127 (introduction to Book IV).

28. See Anthony Blunt, *Art and Architecture in France 1500–1750* (Baltimore: Penguin Books, 1957, 2nd ed.), pp. 93f.

29. *Ibid.*, p. 45.

30. *Ibid.*, p. 188.

31. M. Petzet, "Claude Perrault als Architekt des Pariser Observatoriums," *Zeitschrift für Kunstgeschichte*, Vol. XXX (1967), pp. 1–54.

32. Blunt, *op. cit.*, p. 213.
33. *Ibid.*, p. 214.
34. Haussmann, *Mémoires* (Paris: V. Harvard, 1890–1893), Vol. II, p. 233.

CRITICAL EVALUATION: 2

35. Until the mid-nineteenth century the old city of Vienna was surrounded by a *glacis* (a wide sloping field of fire on which construction was prohibited) similar to that which encircled the 1840 wall of Paris. The outlying *faubourgs* had gradually merged with the surrounding villages, but the outer city remained effectively isolated from the core city. Gradually losing in strategic importance, the *glacis* was converted into a parklike greenbelt in the early nineteenth century—not unlike Napoleon's later scheme. But the breach between the city and the *faubourgs* was too flagrant to remain a permanent fixture. It was into this open space that the Ring development, the Viennese equivalent of Haussmann's Paris, was built from the later 1850's on. The similarities and differences between the developments in Paris and Vienna deserve further study and extended analysis. In any event, it was only when the artificially severed parts were joined that the city was ready to perform the functions required of an urban complex in the second half of the nineteenth century (see Note 8).

PARIS SINCE HAUSSMANN

36. Choay, *op. cit.*
37. Norma Evenson, *Le Corbusier: The Machine and the Grand Design* (Planning and Cities series) (New York: George Braziller, Inc., 1969).
38. For a discussion of the fringe areas with reference to Paris, see G. A. Wissink, *American Cities in Perspective with Special Reference to the Development of Their Fringe Areas* (Assen, 1962), pp. 71f.

DATES OF PERSONS AND REIGNS MENTIONED IN THE TEXT

Monarchs and Reigns (Dates of Rule)	Contemporary Figures (Life Dates)
Constantius Chlorus A.D. 305–306	
Julian the Apostate 361–363	
Merovingian dynasty 481–751	
Carolingian dynasty 751–987	
Hugh Capet 987–996	
Louis VI the Fat 1108–1137	
Philip Augustus 1180–1223	
Louis IX (Saint) 1226–1270	
Philip IV the Fair 1285–1314	
John II the Good 1350–1364	Philip the Bold 1342–1404 (Duke of Burgundy)
Charles V 1364–1380	
Francis I 1515–1547	
Henry II 1547–1559	
Henry III 1574–1589	Marie de Medicis 1573–1642
House of Bourbon 1589–1795	
Henry IV 1589–1610	Cardinal Richelieu 1585–1642
Louis XIII 1610–1643	Cardinal Mazarin 1602–1661
	Jean-Baptiste Colbert 1619–1683
Louis XIV 1643–1715	Jules Hardouin-Mansart 1646–1708
Louis XV 1715–1774	Comte Claude Henri de Saint-Simon 1760–1825
Louis XVI 1774–1793	
Napoleon I 1808–1814	Georges-Eugène Haussmann 1809–1891
Restoration of House of Bourbon 1814–1830	
Louis Philippe 1830–1848 (*July Monarchy–Orléans*)	Jules Ferry 1832–1893
Napoleon III 1852–1871 (*Second Empire*)	

BIBLIOGRAPHY

The literature on Paris, its history and its monuments, is voluminous and specialized. For bibliography on buildings, places, and subjects mentioned in this study, the reader is referred to the *Avery Memorial Architectural Library Catalog* (Boston, 1968), 2nd ed., enlarged, particularly Vol. 14, pp. 261–367, containing literally hundreds of entries arranged by subject. The following brief bibliography, arranged in chronological order, is divided into four parts: (1) the important literature on Haussmann, (2) sources for the history of Paris, (3) modern works on the history of Paris, (4) plans of Paris.

HAUSSMANN'S PARIS

Daly, César. "Les Travaux de Paris," *Revue générale de l'architecture* (Paris, 1862).
Fournel, Victor. *Paris nouveau et Paris futur.* Paris: Lecoffre, 1865. A contemporary view.
Alphand, Adolphe. *Les Promenades de Paris.* Paris, 1867–1873.
Belgrand, Eugène. *Les Travaux souterrains de Paris.* Paris, 1873–1877.
Haussmann, Georges-Eugène. *Memoires du Baron Haussmann.* Paris: V. Havard, 1890–1893.
Bouillat, E. M. *Georges-Eugène Haussmann.* Paris, 1901.
Smith, E. R. "Baron Haussmann and the Topographical Transformation of Paris under Napoleon III," *The Architectural Record*, Vol. XXII (1907), pp. 121–133; 227–238; 369–385; 490–506; Vol. XXIII (1908), pp. 21–38. A detailed study of Haussmann's work set against the background of the history of Paris since its beginnings. Second Empire Paris set up as a model for turn-of-the-century Beaux-Arts architects in America. Dated in viewpoint, but well illustrated.
Halbwachs, Maurice. "Les plans d'extension et d'aménagement de Paris avant le XIXième siècle," *La vie urbaine* (1920). Includes statement of Haussmann's work.
———. *La population et les tracés de voirie à Paris.* Paris: Alcan, 1928.
Peets, E. "Famous Town Planners: Haussmann," *Town Planning Review,* Vol. XII, No. 3 (1927), pp. 187–188. A very brief outline of Haussmann's work.
Mumford, Lewis. *The Culture of Cities.* New York: Harcourt, Brace, and World, 1938.
Giedion, Sigfried. *Space, Time and Architecture*, Cambridge, Mass.: Harvard University Press, 1941 and later editions. The most significant modern statement and critique of Haussmann's project.
Pillement, G. *Destruction de Paris.* Paris, c. 1941. Critical of Haussmann demolitions.
Girard, Louis. *La politique des travaux publics du second Empire.* Paris, A. Colin, 1952. Political implications of Paris transformation.
Réau, L., Lavedan, P., et al. *L'Oeuvre du Baron Haussmann, Préfet de la Seine (1853–1870).* Paris, 1954. Well-illustrated summary, but undefined in its critical evaluation of Haussmann's work.
Chapman, J. M. and B. *The Life and Times of Baron Haussmann; Paris in the Second Empire.* London, 1957. Popular account.

Pinkney, David H. *Napoleon III and the Rebuilding of Paris.* Princeton: University Press, 1958. Excellent scholarly account of Haussmann's work with critical evaluation of political and economic factors involved. Extensive bibliography.

HISTORY OF PARIS: SOURCES

Félibien, Dom Michel. *Histoire de la Ville de Paris.* Paris, 1685–1688.
De la Force, J. Piganiol. *Description de Paris.* Paris, 1736.
Lebeuf, Abbé Jean. *Histoire de la ville et de tout le diocèse de Paris.* Paris, 1754–1758 (3rd ed., Paris, 1883–1892).
Jaillot, J. B. *Réchérches critiques, historiques et topographiques sur la ville de Paris depuis ses commencements connus jusqu'a présent.* Paris, 1775.
Berty, A. et al., *Topographie historique du vieux Paris.* Paris, 1866–1897.

HISTORY OF PARIS: MODERN WORKS

Halphen, L. *Paris sous les premiers Capétiens (987–1223), études de topographie historique.* Paris, 1909.
De Pachtère, F.-G. *Paris à l'époque gallo romaine.* Paris, 1912.
Jullian, C. *Le Paris des Romains.* Paris, 1924.
Poëte, M. *Une vie de cité: Paris de sa naissance à nos jours.* Paris, 1924.
Franklin, A. *Paris et les Parisiens au XVIe siècle.* Paris, 1921.
Dumolin, M. *Etudes de topographie parisienne.* Paris, 1929–1931.
Barroux, R. *Paris dès origines à nos jours et son rôle dans l'histoire de la civilisations.* Paris, 1951.
Rochegude, Marquis de, and Clébert, J.-P. *Le rues de Paris.* Paris, 1958.
Cheronnet, L. *Paris tel qui'l fut; 104 photographies anciens.* Paris, n.d.
Laffont, Robert ed., *An Illustrated History of Paris and the Parisians.* New York, 1958.
Friedmann, Abbé. *Paris: ses rues, ses paroisses du moyen age a la revolution. Origine et évolution des circonscriptions paroissiales.* Paris, 1959.
Hillairet, J. *Connaissance du vieux Paris.* Paris, 1963, 3 vols.
———. *Dictionnaire historique des rues de Paris.* Paris, 1963, 2 vols.
  Streets listed alphabetically by name with a wealth of topographical information.
Speckter, H. *Paris: Städtebau von der Renaissance bis zur Neuzeit.* Munich, 1964.

PARIS: PLANS

Bonnardot, A. *Etudes archeologiques sur les anciens plans de Paris des XVIe, XVIIe et XVIIIe siècles.* Paris, 1851.
Franklin, A. *Les anciens plans de Paris, notices historiques et topographiques.* Paris, 1878.
Atlas des anciens plans de Paris. Paris, 1880. 3 vols.

INDEX

Numbers in roman refer to pages; those in *italics* refer to illustrations. Unless otherwise indicated, all entries that refer to the functions or parts of a city pertain to Paris. The reader is referred to *Fig. 18* for a schematic plan, which depicts the major urban features of Paris discussed in the text. Names of individual avenues, boulevards, bridges, streets, parks, and railways, for example, have been indexed under the appropriate group heading.

Alberti, Leon Battista, 34, 35, 119n.25, 119n.27
Alphand, Adolphe, 11, 19, 118n.3
Anne of Austria, 38, 39
apartment buildings. *See* housing
aqueducts. *See* water supply
Arc de Triomphe, *Fig. 76*; 17, 44
architects, in Haussmann's period, 18, 26
Arènes de Lutèce, 29
arrondissements, 17, 114, 115
Asnières, collectors' sewers, 20
Avenues: de Champs-Elysées, *Figs. 66, 75–76*; 42, 43, 44
    de l'Impératrice (now Ave. Foch), *Fig. 25*
    Napoleon (now Ave. de l'Opéra), 15
    de l'Opéra (formerly Ave. Napoleon), *Fig. 16*; 15
    Wagram, 114
    See also Boulevards; maps and views of Paris; streets, plan of

Baltard, Victor, *Fig. 22*; 18
Barcelona, 25
Baroque style, 6, 16, 40, 41, 43
Bastille, the, *Fig. 43*; 14–15, 33, 43. Colonne de la Bastille, 17
Batignolles, Les, 114
"Beaubourg," the, 30
Beauharnais, Prince Eugène, 13
Belgrand, Eugène, 11, 20, 118n.3
Berlin, 25
Bibliothèque du Roi, *Fig. 63*
Bibliothèque Nationale, 18
Bishop of Paris, 29, 32
Bordeaux, 12
Boulevards: Henri IV, 17
    Malesherbes, 15, 114
    Pereire, 114
    Poissonière, *Fig. 78*
    Raspail, 15
    Richard-Lenoir, *Fig. 87*
    St.-Germain, 15, 17
    Sébastopol, *Fig. 20*; 17
    See also Avenues; maps and views of Paris; streets, plan of
Boullée, Étienne, 9
Bourbon, Palais, *Fig. 72*
Bourbon Restoration, 11, 12, 13, 44
Bourg-le-Abbé, 30

Bourg-Neuf Saint-Germain, 30
Bourg Saint-Germain-des-Prés, *Fig. 33*; 36
Bourg Saint-Germain-l'Auxerrois, 30, 119n.22
Bourg Sainte-Geneviève, *Fig. 33*
bourgeoisie. *See* social classes
Bourse, the, *Fig. 63*; 17, 41
Bretonvilliers, Hôtel de, *Fig. 43*; 36
bridges, *Fig. 34*; Roman, *Fig. 34*; 29. Stone (by Louis XIV), 40; wooden (seventeenth-century), 40.
    Grand Pont (now Pont-au-Change), *Fig. 34*; 29, 30, 33
    Petit Pont, *Figs. 19, 20, 34, 53*; 29, 33
    Pont d'Archevêche, *Fig. 20*
    d'Arcole, *Fig. 20*
    -au-Change (formerly Grand Pont), *Figs. 20, 34*
    de la Concorde, *Figs. 71, 72*; 43, 44
    au Double, *Fig. 20*
    Louis-Philippe, *Fig. 20*
    Marie, *Figs. 20, 43*; 36
    Neuf, *Figs. 19, 46*; 17–18, 36, 40
    Notre-Dame, *Fig. 20*
    Royal, 40
    St.-Michel, *Fig. 20*
    Sully, *Figs. 20, 49*; 17
    de la Tournelle, *Figs. 20, 43*; 36
Brosse, Salomon de, *Fig. 52*
Bruant, Libéral, *Figs. 57, 62*
Brunelleschi, Filippo, 34, 119n.25
Burgundians, the, 33

Caisse des Travaux, 21
Canal de l'Ourc, *Fig. 59*; 44
Capet, Hugh, 29
Carolingians, the, 29, 30, 32
Catherine de Medicis, 38
cemeteries, *Fig. 30*; 19–20.
    Cimetière Montmartre (formerly Cim. du Nord), *Fig. 30*; 20
    Montparnasse (formerly Cim. du Sud), *Fig. 30*
    du Nord (now Cim. Montmartre), *Fig. 30*
    Père Lachaise, *Fig. 30*; 20
    des Saints-Innocents, *Figs. 34, 40*; 30, 32
    du Sud (now Cim. Montparnasse), *Fig. 30*
Chaillot hill, *Fig. 66*; 42
Champ-de-Mars, *Fig. 67*; 25, 42

Champlain, Samuel de, 39
Charles V, *Fig. 35*; 33, 35, 37, 38, 40, 41
Chartreux, Couvent de, 40
Chastillon, Claude, *Fig. 45*
Chaux, *Figs. 5–6*; 10
CIAM (Congrès Internationaux d'Architecture Moderne) theories of city planning, 25
Colbert, Jean Baptiste, 40
Collège de Navarre, 44
Collège des Quatre Nations (now the Palais de l'Institut de France), 39
commercial centers, 15, 23, 30, 35, 41, 116
Communards, the, 33
Constantius Chlorus, 29; the Baths of, *Fig. 31*
Cours-la-Reine, 43
Crédit Foncier, 22
Crédit Mobilier, 21, 22

Debucourt, P. L., *Fig. 36*
Dentzel, General Georges, 13
Deschamps, 15, 22
Dhuis, river valley, 20
Duban, F.-J., 18
Durand, J.-N.-L., 9

East Indies, the, 39
École des Beaux-Arts, 18
École Militaire, *Fig. 67*; 42
École Polytechnique, 18, 44
Eiffel Tower, *Fig. 76*; 25
England, 8, 33; *see also* London
Escorial, the, 39

faubourgs, 15, 30–31, 32, 38, 40
Faubourg Saint-Germain, 36, 40, 42
Faubourg Saint-Honoré, *Figs. 50, 54, 66*; 38, 40
Ferry, Jules, 20, 118n.7
Florence, 34, 119n.25
floods, reduction of, 20
Fontaine, Pierre François L., *Figs. 72–73*; 9
fortifications, *Fig. 54*; 29, 33, 35, 37, 38, 46; *see also* the Bastille; walls of Paris
François I, 37, 38, 40, 116
Friedmann, Abbé, *Fig. 33*, 119n.22

Gabriel, Jacques-Ange, *Fig. 68*; 42
Garnier, Charles, *Fig. 84*; 16, 18
Garnier, Tony, 25
Gärtner, Friedrich von, 9
German troops entering Paris (1870), *Fig. 2*
Giedion, Sigfried, *Fig. 87*; 26, 118n.13–19
Gobelin weavers, 40
Gothic architecture, 18, 31

Halles, Les. *See* markets
Hardouin-Mansart, Jules, *Figs. 62, 64*; 40–41
Harclay, Achille de, 35
Haussmann, Georges-Eugène, *Fig. 1*; 10–11, 14–15, 19, 44, 112, 115–116; aesthetics of, 16–19; as administrator, 13, 15–16, 18–19; background of, 13, 21; character, 13, 21; criticism of, 20–21, 25–28, 112; demise, 20–21, 48; economic ideas, 20–23; education, 13, 28; influence of, 25, 118n.8; *Mémoires*, 11; reconstruction of Paris: apartment houses, 26–27, 115; architecture, 18; boulevards, 16–17, 26; bridges, *Fig. 49*; cemeteries, 20; lighting, 19–20; parks, 19; the old city, 27; sewers, 20; street plans, 26, 37; water system, 20
Hénard, Eugène, 117
Henry II, 35, 37, 40
Henry III, 36
Henry IV, 34, 35, 36, 37, 39, 40, 41
highways, 26, 117
Hittorf, J.-I., *Fig. 69*; 43
hospitals, 17, 32. Hôtel Dieu, *Figs. 19, 53*; 17, 32, 39. Hospice des Quinze-Vingts, *Fig. 50*; 32, 38. Hôpital de la Salpêtrière, *Fig. 57*; 39
Hôtel de Bretonvilliers, *Fig. 43*; 36
Hôtel Dieu. *See* hospitals
Hôtel de Ville, *Figs. 12, 42, 49*; 16, 17, 18, 33, 44
Hôtel des Invalides, *Fig. 62*; 40
Hôtel des Tournelles, 35
Hôtel St.-Pol, 37
housing, 27, 35, 47, 112–113; apartment buildings, *Figs. 32, 82*; 17, 23, 26–27, 36, 115; *see also* residential areas
Hugo, Victor, 18; house of, *Fig. 44*
Hundred Years War, 33

Ile de la Cité, *Figs. 19, 20, 34, 37, 38*; 14, 17, 29, 34, 36, 37, 40
Ile de Notre Dame (now Ile Saint-Louis), *Figs. 34, 37*
Ile Saint-Louis (formerly Ile de Notre Dame), *Figs. 12, 34, 43, 49*; 36, 47
Ile de Louviers, *Fig. 37*
Industrial Revolution, 10, 11
International Exposition (1889), *Fig. 76*

Jacquerie uprisings, 34
Jefferson, Thomas, 8, 9, 10
John II the Good, 33
Julian the Apostate, 29

July Monarchy, 11–12, 14, 43, 46; *see also* Louis Philippe
Junie plan of Paris (1783), *Fig. 34*

Karlsruhe, Germany, *Figs. 3–5*; 9–10
Knights of the Temple (Templiers), *Figs. 34, 47*; 30, 35

Labrouste, Henri, 18, 25
Le Corbusier, 25, 27, 117
Ledoux, Claude-Nicolas, *Fig. 75*; 9. See also Chaux
Left Bank, the, 14–15, 29, 31, 32, 36
Lefuel, H. M., *Fig. 21*; 18
legitimists, 113
Le Nôtre, André, 42
Leonardo da Vinci, 34, 119n.25
Lescot, Pierre, 37
lighting, 19–20
Limbourg brothers, *Fig. 38*
London, *Fig. 13*; 14, 16, 115.
Longchamps racetrack, 19
Louis VI the Fat, 30
Louis IX (Saint), 32, 38
Louis XIII, *Fig. 54*; 36, 38, 39
Louis XIV, 15, 18, 37, 38, 39, 40, 41, 42, 47
Louis XV, *Fig. 39*; 18, 37, 42, 43
Louis XVI, *Fig. 70*; 43
Louis Napoleon, 13
Louis Philippe, *Fig. 49*; 11–12, 44; *see also* July Monarchy; Orléans régime
Louvre, the, *Figs. 21, 34, 50*; 15, 16, 17, 18, 33, 37–39, 40, 41, 42, 44, 116
Lutetia Parisiorum, 29
Lyons, 12

Madeleine, La, *Figs. 69, 74*; 17, 43, 44
maps and views of Paris, *Figs. 7, 12, 30, 35, 37, 43, 54, 59, 76, 77*; 14, 15
Marais quarter, 35, 37
Marcel, Étienne, 33, 37
Marché des Champeaux. *See* markets
Mare d'Auteuil, Bois de Boulogne, *Fig. 24*
Marie, Christopher, 36
Marie de Medicis, 38
markets, *Fig. 48*; 29, 30, 34, 36; Les Halles, *Figs. 22, 33–34*; 12, 15, 17, 18, 25, 30, 41. Marché des Champeaux (later Les Halles), *Fig. 33*; St.-Germaine-des-Prés, Foire, *Fig. 37*; St.-Germaine-des-Prés, markets, *Fig. 48*
Marseilles, 12
Martin, Pierre Denis, *Fig. 39*
Mazarin, Cardinal, 39
Merian view of Paris (1620), *Figs. 35, 54*
Merovingians, the, 29

Méry-sur-Oise, 20
monarchists, 11
Mumford, Lewis, 25

Napoleon I, *Figs. 59, 72–73*; 8, 9, 11, 18, 20, 43
Napoleon III, *Figs. 1, 7, 11*; 8, 10–11, 12–13, 14, 16, 18–19, 20, 23, 26, 27, 28, 37, 47, 112, 116, 118n.7, 122; *see also* the Second Empire
Nash, John, 9, 14
National Assembly, the, 17
Neuilly, 114
Normans, the, 29
Notre Dame Cathedral, *Figs. 19, 20, 53*; 16, 17, 18, 31, 32

Observatoire, the, *Figs. 60–61*; 15, 40, 119n.31
Opéra, the, *Fig. 84*; 15, 17, 18
Orléans, 30
Orléans régime, 12, 13; ex-Orléanists, 113. *see also* Louis Phillipe
Oudrey, Jean-Baptiste, *Fig. 53*

Pagniez, Gustave, 119n.26
Palais Bourbon, *Fig. 72*
Palais-Cardinal (renamed Palais-Royal, 1642), 38
Palais de Justice, *Fig. 20*; 17
Palais de Tuileries, *Figs. 35, 50–51, 66*; 37, 38, 42
Palais du Luxembourg, *Fig. 52*; 38
Palais Mazarin, *Fig. 63*; 41
Palais-Royal (formerly Palais-Cardinal), *Figs. 19, 38, 50*; 38–39, 41, 116; gardens, *Fig. 63*; 117
Palladio, Andrea, 35, 119n.27
Panthéon, (formerly Ste. Geneviève church), *Figs. 49, 76*; 17
parishes, Parisian (c. 1292), *Fig. 34*
parks, 11, 18–19, 116.
 Bois de Boulogne, *Figs. 23–25*; 19, 42
 Bois de Vincennes, *Fig. 26*; 19
 Jardin du Luxembourg, 14–15
 Jardins des Tuileries, *Figs. 66, 71*; 39, 42, 43
 Jardin du Roi, *Fig. 34*
 Parc des Buttes Chaumont, 19
 Parc de Monceau, 19, 114, 115
 Parc Montsouris, 19
parlement, the, 32, 35
Percier, Charles, *Figs. 72, 73*; 9
Pereire, Émile and Isaac, 19, 21, 115
Perrault, Charles, *Fig. 60*
Persigny, Duc de, 13

125

Petit Chatelet, *Fig. 19*
Philip Augustus, *Fig. 34*; 31–32, 33, 39, 41
Philip the Bold, 33
Philip IV the Fair, 32
Pinkney, David, 7, 11, 118n.2, 118n.6, 122
Place: de la Concorde, *Figs. 68–72*; 15, 38, 42, 43, 44
    Dauphine, *Figs. 19, 35, 46*; 17, 34, 35, 36
    de l'Étoile (now Place de Charles de Gaulle), 14, 15, 42, 44, 114, 116
    de France, *Figs. 45, 47*; 34, 35, 36–37, 119n.26
    de Grève, *Figs. 34, 41*; 29–30, 33
    Louis XV (now Place de la Concorde), 42–44
    de la Madeleine, *Fig. 69;* 43
    de la Nation, 16, 116
    du Parvis, *Fig. 20;* 18
    de la Revolution (formerly Place Louis XV, now Place de la Concorde), 43
    Royale, by Henri IV (now Place des Vosges), *Figs. 43–44*; 34, 35, 37
    Royale, by Louis XIV (now Place Vendôme), *Fig. 35*; 41
    des Ternes, 115
    Vendôme (formerly Place Royale by Louis XIV), *Figs. 65, 72*; 42, 44
    des Victoires, *Figs. 63–64*; 40–41
    des Vosges (formerly Place Royale by Henri IV), *Figs. 35, 43–44*; 115
    See also Square of Henry IV; Square of Louis XIV
Plaine de Grenelle, 42
Plateau de Gravelle, *Fig. 26*
Police, Prefecture du, *Fig. 20*; 17
population growth, 9–10
Porte: de Buci, 36
    Dauphine, *Fig. 25*
    d'Orléans, 15
    Saint-Antoine, *Fig. 43*; 33
    Saint-Denis, 41
    Saint-Honoré, *Fig. 34*; 33, 38
    du Temple, *Fig. 47*; 39

Railways, *Fig. 59*; 12, 14, 16, 17, 20, 25, 44–45, 116.
    Gare de l'Est (formerly Strasbourg terminal), *Fig. 76*; 14, 15
    Gare de Montparnasse, 15
    Gare du Nord, *Fig. 76*; 15
    Gare St. Lazare, *Fig. 8*
    Strasbourg terminal (now Gare de l'Est), *Fig. 9*
Rambuteau, Count de, 44
Renaissance, the, 9, 34–35, 119n.25

Republicans, the, 113
residential centers, 17, 23, 35, 41, 47, 116; *see also* housing
restaurants, 14, 114; Café Moulin Rouge, *Fig. 86*; Restaurant Pied-de-Mouton, *Fig. 85*
Revolution of 1848, *Fig. 10*; 12
Richelieu, Cardinal, 38, 39
Right Bank, the, 29, 30, 32, 40, 44
Roman: apartment houses, 115; Arènes de Lutèce, 29; bridges and roads, 29–30; Baths of Constantius Chlorus, *Fig. 31*
Romanesque style, 31
Rome, 25, 34; Piazza del Popolo, 36
Rond Point, the, 42
Rothschilds, the, 21

Saalman, Howard, 119n.24, 119n.25
St.-Denis, abbey, *Fig. 59*; 29, 30
St.-Eustache, church, 41
St.-Germain-des-Prés, abbey, *Figs. 34, 37*; 15, 16, 29, 30, 32
St.-Germain-des-Prés, Foire and markets. *See* markets
St.-Germain-l'Auxerrois, church, *Fig. 34*; 37
St.-Gervais, church, *Figs. 34, 39*; 30
St.-Jacques-la-Boucherie, church, *Figs. 34, 40*; 17, 30
Saint Louis. *See* Louis IX
St.-Louis, chapel of, 40
St.-Louis, Ile. *See* Ile Saint-Louis
St.-Magloire, monastery, *Fig. 34*; 30
St.-Martin-des-Champs, *Fig. 34*; 30
St.-Merry, church, *Fig. 34*; 30
St.-Opportune, church, 30
St.-Pol, Hôtel. *See* Hôtel St.-Pol
Saint-Simon, Comte Claude Henri de, 12
Saint-Simonists, 21, 22
St.-Sulpice, church, *Fig. 48*
St.-Victor, Abbey, 39
Ste.-Chapelle, *Figs. 20, 38–39*; 32
Ste-Geneviève, church, 29, 32; *see also* the Pantheon
Ste.-Madeleine, church, 42–43
Schinkel, Karl Friedrich, 9
Second Empire, the, 10, 13, 15, 16–17, 20, 23–24, 25–26, 29, 47, 48, 112–113; *see also* Napoleon III
Senlis, 30
Serlio, Sebastiano, 35
Service d'Architecture, 18
Service du Plan de Paris, 15
sewers, *Figs. 27, 29–30*; 11, 19–20, 46, 116; *see also* water supply

Smith, Adam, 31, 119n.23
social classes: lower (the urban proletariat; working classes), 11, 12, 19, 23, 26–27, 34, 36, 46–47, 116; lower middle (*petite bourgeoisie*), 12, 34, 47, 112, 116; middle (bourgeoisie), 9, 10, 11, 23, 26–27, 30, 31, 32, 34, 47, 48, 112, 116; upper middle (*haute bourgeoisie*), 12, 14, 16, 23–24, 25–26, 34, 40, 47. 48, 112, 113; upper, 34, 35, 41, 116; revolutions, bourgeois, 8, 9, 33
socialists, 11, 12, 13, 119n.20
Sorbonne, the, *Fig. 55*; 39
Square of Henry IV, 47
Square of Louis XIV, 47
stores, 14, 34, 36, 114; confectioner's shop, *Fig. 83*; Magasin du Grand Colbert, *Fig. 79*; Maison du Bon Marché, *Fig. 80*
streets, plan of, *Figs. 7, 15, 17*; 14–17, 22–23, 26–27, 36–37, 41, 44, 47, 113–116.
    Grant Rue, La (later Rue St. Denis), *Fig. 34*
    Rue d'Aboukir (formerly Rue des Fossés Mont-martre), *Fig. 64*; 41
    d'Anjou, 37
    du Bac, *Fig. 80*; 40
    de Beaune, 40
    de Boucherat (formerly Rue-Neuve Saint-Louis, now Rue de Turenne), *Fig. 47*
    de Castiglione, *Fig. 72*; 44
    Champs-Elysées (now Rue Boissy d'Anglas), 43
    Charlot, *Fig. 47*; 36–37
    de Cléry, 41
    de Courcelles, 115
    Croix des Petits-Champs, 41
    Dauphine, 36
    des Écoles, 15
    du Faubourg-Montmartre, *Fig. 78*
    du Faubourg Saint-Honoré, 41, 43, 115
    des Fossés Mont-martre (now Rue d'Aboukir), *Fig. 64*
    des Fossés Saint-Germain, 30
    des Halles, 15
    Lafayette, 15
    des Lavandières, 30
    du Mail, 41
    Neuve des Petits-Champs, *Figs. 64, 72, 79*; 41, 44
    Neuve Saint-Louis (later Rue de Boucherat, now Rue de Turenne), 37
    de Pont Neuf, 15
    des Pyramides, *Fig. 72*; 44
    du 4 Septembre, 15
    de Rambuteau, *Fig. 14*; 12, 14
    de Rennes, 15
    de Richelieu, *Figs. 50, 63*; 39, 40, 117
    de Rivoli, *Figs. 71–72*; 14, 44, 47
    Royale, *Fig. 74*; 15, 17, 43, 47
    St.-Antoine, *Fig. 10*; 14
    St.-Florentin, 43
    St.-Honoré, *Fig. 69*; 15, 37, 38
    St.-Martin, *Fig. 34*; 14, 29
    St.-Nicaise, *Fig. 50*
    de Sèvres, *Fig. 80*
    Soufflot, 15
    de Turbigo, 15
    de Turenne, *Fig. 47*
    Vauvilliers, *Fig. 85*
suburbs, 112, 115, 116; "greenbelt" project, 26, 112; industrial, 40
Sully, Duc de, 35
surveying, of Paris, 15; *see also* Deschamps

Templiers. *See* Knights of the Temple
Texier, Edmond, *Figs. 8–9, 12, 27, 56, 60, 69, 78–79, 81–83*
theaters, 9, 17; Théâtre-Lyrique, *Fig. 81*
Tour de Nesle, 39
trade guilds, 31; trade unions, 16
traffic, 116–117
transportation, public, 43, 116; *see also* railways
Tribunal de Commerce, *Fig. 20*; 16, 17
Turgot plan of Paris (1734), *Figs. 19, 43, 47, 50, 63–64*

Université, the, 17

Val-de-Grâce, abbey, *Figs. 58, 76*; 39
Vanne, river valley, 20
Versailles, *Fig. 59*; 40
Vienna, 25
Viollet-le-Duc, Eugène Emmanuel, 18
Visconti, L.-T.-J., 18

walls of Paris, *Figs. 34–35, 37, 77*; 14, 29, 30–33, 34, 35, 38, 39, 40, 41, 44, 119n.22
water supply, 11, 19–20, 44, 116; Yonne aqueduct, *Fig. 28*
Weinbrenner, Friedrich, 9
working classes. *See* social classes
Wren, Christopher, *Fig. 13*; 14, 16

Yonne, river valley, 20; aqueduct, *Fig. 28*

SOURCES OF ILLUSTRATIONS

Adolphe Alphand, *Les Promenades de Paris* (Paris, 1867–1873), plate volume: 24–26, 52
Architecture et la Décoration aux Palais du Louvre et des Tuileries, pl. LX:21
Eugéne Belgrand, *Travaux souterains de Paris* (Paris, 1873–1877): 28 (vol. V), 29 (vol. IV), 30 (vol. V, atlas)
Leonardo Benevolo, *Storia dell'Architettura Moderna* (Bari, 1960), fig. 74: 77
Bibliothèque Nationale, Paris: 2, 42, 48, 67, 75
Bolton, Arthur T., and H. Duncan Hendry, eds., *The Wren Society* (Oxford, 1935), vol. XII, pl. 25: 13
J.E. Bulloz, Paris: 36, 39, 40, 44, 53, 73
L. Cheronnet, *Paris tel qu'il fut; 104 photographies anciens* (Paris, n.d.), pl. 95: 85
Jean-Paul Clébert, *Les Rues de Paris* (Paris, 1958), pl. 156: 68 (above and below)
George R. Collins: 76
Courtauld Institute of Art, London: 45
Abbé Friedmann, *Paris. Ses rues, ses paroisses du môyen age à la révolution* (Paris, 1959): 33, 34
Sigfried Giedion, *Space, Time and Architecture* (Cambridge, Mass., Harvard University Press, copyright 1962 by the President and Fellows of Harvard College): 16, 66, 87
Giraudon, Paris: 38, 51
Werner Hegemann and Elbert Peets, *The American Vitruvius: An Architect's Handbook of Civic Art* (New York, 1922), pl. 1027: 7
R. Henrard, Paris: 20, 49, 57, 58, 61–62, 71
Fred Hill, New York: 18
Robert Laffont, *Paris and Its People, an Illustrated History* (London, 1958): 1, 10, 11, 17, 41, 59, 70, 80, 84, 86
Claude-Nicolas Ledoux, *L'Architecture considerée sous le rapport de l'Art, des Moeurs et de la legislation* (Paris, 1804): 5, 6
David H. Pinkney, *Napoleon III and the Rebuilding of Paris* (Princeton, 1958): 15, 22, 23, 32 (all reprinted by permission of Princeton University Press)
Howard Saalman: 14, 35, 37, 54, 74
Service Photographique des Musées Nationaux, Versailles: 31
Edward R. Smith, "Baron Haussmann and the Topographical Transformation of Paris under Napoléon III," *The Architectural Record*, XXII (1907), p. 373: 72
Edmond Texier, *Tableau de Paris* (Paris, 1852): 8–9, 12, 27, 55, 56, 60, 69, 78–79, 81–83
Michel Turgot, *Plan de Paris* (1734): 19, 43, 47, 50, 63, 64
University of California, Berkeley, Library Photographic Service: 65
Arthur Valdenaire, *Friedrich Weinbrenner. Sein Leben und Seine Bauten* (Karlsruhe, 1919), pls. 79, 111: 3, 4